Successful

Log Homes

Successful

Log Homes

Planning & Building, Renovating & Repairing

James D. Ritchie

Structures Publishing Company
Farmington, Michigan

Manufactured in the United States of America

Edited by Shirley H. Horowitz

Cover photos courtesy Vermont Log Buildings and the author

Book design by Carey Jean Ferchland

Current Printing (last digit)
10   9   8   7   6   5   4   3   2   1

Library of Congress Cataloging in Publication Data

Ritchie, James D
  Successful log houses.

  Bibliography: p.
  Includes index.
  1. Log cabins.   I. Title.
TH4840.R57   690'.8'7   78-15308
ISBN 0-912336-71-4
ISBN 0-912336-72-2 pbk.

Contents

Modern design and construction techniques have taken the log home well out of the ''cabin'' category. This 3,190-square-foot home near Forest Lake, Minnesota, has five bedrooms, three bathrooms and three-car garage. The house was designed and factory-built by Boyne Falls Log Homes Company.

INTRODUCTION

You apparently have more than a casual interest in log buildings and their construction: you are reading this book. And, if you are seriously considering a log construction project—whether from scratch, with a kit, or recycling an older building,—this book has been written specifically for you.

Whether your undertaking will result in a two-room cabin on the shore of a mountain lake, or a full-time family dwelling with hundreds of square feet of living space, the construction principles are the same. Whether you build this year or ten years from now, the information we have collected and arranged on log construction will be as timely. Whether you will build your house from logs you cut and hew by hand, or from a precut factory kit, we have outlined time- and money-saving techniques you will find valuable.

You are in strong company if you're planning your own log home. A growing number of home owners find log construction fascinating and log homes thoroughly livable—and more than three-quarters of the builders do a major part of the work themselves.

What is it about a log house that is so universally appealing? For many, an old log cabin is one of the more exciting sights along a country road. And this appeal survives time and weather. The ruins of few frame structures, regardless of the former magnificence of the house, stir nearly the same chords that respond to the sight of a log home, no matter what the wind, rain and years have done to the building.

The main interest of a log house may be rooted in admiration of the crafts of our pioneer forefathers who, with crude tools and their own two hands, hewed the forest into homes for their families. Some of us have close ties to that kind of history—I spent my first two years on earth, only forty summers ago, in a two-rooms-and-a-loft log house in south-central Missouri. My memory of the house is only second-hand, but I cling happily to it.

The log cabin is truly the "folk house" of America, and exploring one built years ago is like turning back the pages of history. And nowadays log homes are making a strong comeback, with truly modern structures that are comfortable, functional and attractive. New developments in materials and technology have taken the log home out of the history books and into an up-to-date housing category. Whatever the basic attraction of log houses to modern-day builders, this type of whole-wood construction has a fundamental beauty — proportion, balance and strength — that allows each builder to make his own unique statement of self-expression.

Do-it-yourselfers who enjoy a challenge are cutting their own logs and building their homes — in both rustic and urban settings. The styles and construction techniques employed in these "from-scratch" log homes are as individual as the builders themselves.

Factory-cut and prefabricated log homes are gaining wide acceptance also. Through modern machinery and manufacturing methods, precut and prefab log homes can be quickly assembled on the site, creating handsome weathertight dwellings. Log home companies (more of them keep appearing all the time) are scattered from coast to coast. Many of them have several milling locations and nationwide distribution systems. Several will cut materials to suit about any style and design of home the customer wishes to build.

Log construction definitely has moved beyond the "cabin" category. And, while the basic structural methods and materials are different, the principles of building with logs remain the same as building with any other material:

(1) build according to an efficient, well-thought-out plan, on a well-chosen site;
(2) use top-quality materials;
(3) use sound construction techniques.

In the chapters ahead you will find designs of and plans for successful log homes, both those built from raw logs and those constructed from precut logs and prefabricated kits. We provide information on materials and building practices, with tips to guide you through construction from planning to plumbing.

Where possible, we have included information on costs. With the inflation of the past several years, however, estimating costs is a hazardous enterprise, particularly over any kind of time span. Often, lumberyards, mills and building materials suppliers can only make a firm price quote on material they have in inventory. Anything to be ordered is subject to price increases from the factory or wholesaler. Where prices are quoted, we do so with a date reference, so readers may judge how construction costs have changed from that time.

Our goal in preparing this book is to help the prospective log home builder realize the greatest return possible in satisfaction, comfort and value for his investment in thought, time and money.

1.

WHY BUILD WITH LOGS TODAY?

Durability

There were few journeymen carpenters — and even fewer architects — in the vanguard of civilization as it spread from east to west across the North American continent. The frontiersmen were hunters, loggers, traders, trappers and miners, and staying alive was their first concern. They understandably were rather casual about comfort, and even more indifferent to beauty and style in housing. Pioneer cabins were necessarily built of materials readily at hand, and expediency was the rule.

Although the pioneer cabin was not pretentious and often barely comfortable, it had the kind of genuine architectural beauty that reflected the surroundings and way of life of its builder. In those structures that survive, each cabin carries the marks of its builder; the personality of the owner can almost be read in the remains of the house he built.

Some frontiersmen built their cabins rudely and in obvious haste, as if the building was intended to be only a temporary way station on the road west. Other owners took more time and care in fitting notches and joints to provide a warm, durable home with a more permanent attitude. Log homes of cedar, pine, spruce, poplar, chestnut and oak still stand; many are older than the nation. The cedar buildings constructed by French trappers and Jesuit missionaries in the Great Lakes region of the U.S. and Canada are perfectly sound today, more than 200 years after they were built. In fact, a good many of them are still in use.

Today's log home builders appreciate the durability and simple beauty of whole-wood construction — perhaps even more than their cabin-building forefathers did. And while our pioneering ancestors had little choice in the materials from which to build their houses, that is hardly true of their descendents. In fact, the selection of building products is so wide that even builders of conventional homes may have trouble deciding which to use. Plywood, board-and-batten, composition, asphalt or aluminum siding? Cedar shakes, asphalt shingles, tile

This 1880's-built Florida cabin has no windows; however, the doors are exactly opposite each other to let a breeze blow through the house. Corners are held together with large wooden pegs. The original mud-and-stick chimney washed away; the stones shown here were added to replace it. (Photo courtesy the Junior Museum of Bay County, Florida).

or slate roofs? With such a variety of man-made and man-altered building materials, why go back to whole logs as a basic construction product?

Quality Materials

Happily, the use of logs as a main structural material can be combined with modern building products in other features of the home to produce an overall structure that is far superior to anything the 19th century pioneer could build. Foundations of concrete or masonry provide more solid underpinnings for modern log homes than the few flat rocks used by frontiersmen. Roofing materials today are immensely improved over the shingles (called "boards") split by hand from sections of tree trunks. Carpets, linoleum and hardwood floors are vastly superior to the packed dirt or split logs that served in pioneer cabins.

The selection among manufactured materials today allows mixing and matching that preserves and complements the basic charm and character of a log home. This natural warmth and beauty of log construction is the guiding characteristic of many homeowners who choose a log home.

Individuality

"I think more people today want a home that is distinctive; different from other houses in the neighborhood," says Rod Hayes, of Belding and Hayes, Inc., distributors of Beaver Log Homes. "That may explain why we are seeing more urban homeowners build with logs. They reflect their individuality in the kind of home they build."

These homeowners do not build with logs just to be different, or merely to live in an attention-getting "gimmick" of a house, Hayes maintains. They look for style and function in the home designs they choose.

"The majority of our customers design their own homes, or modify one of our standard plans to suit their

Joining faces of logs often were squared with an adze, or broadaxe, to make a tighter-fitting cabin wall.

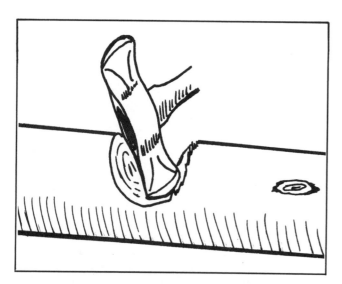

Most early cabins were built of round logs utilizing notched corners. This type of corner is the easiest and fastest to construct. A rounded notch is cut in each log to a depth of half the diameter so that it fits into the log that lays at right angles to it.

A froe and mallet were used to make shakes or "boards" for roofing pioneer cabins. Some old-timers say shakes should be split in the dark of the moon, so they will not warp and curl on the roof.

family's needs," he observes. "They don't just want a house built of logs, they want their own taste and personality to be reflected in a thoroughly livable home. Logs are a versatile building material, and can be used in virtually any design or location."

Urban Settings

As Hayes notes, many people formerly considered log homes appropriate only for rustic, wooded settings. Some still do. And there is a charm and character about a log home that makes it seem particularly suited to building sites in the deep woods, along lake shores or in mountain settings. A log house nestles into these surroundings as if it truly belonged there.

But more and more log homes are going up in towns and residential subdivisions, too, where they contrast with houses of more conventional materials. The versatility Hayes mentions is one major reason why, in this age of contemporary design and styling, many urban home builders elect log construction as a way to express themselves. The contrast of the rustic log exterior with contemporary comfort and easy maintenance indoors combines the best of tradition with modern style and function.

Costs and Workload Options

As with appearance, cost can vary widely with a log home. A precut kit, trucked many miles to the building site and erected with hired professional labor will cost as much as — or more than — a conventional house of the same size and general style. On the other hand, a home builder with the time, talent and timber can build a thoroughly comfortable log home from scratch at a fraction of the cost of a conventional house.

For builders whose main objective is saving money on construction, the do-it-yourself log home has opportunities unequaled in most other methods of building, especially if the builder owns a tract of timber. However, an owner who fells and hews logs from timber on his property trades a lot of his time and hard work to keep the extra dollars in his pocket.

Modern-day "dog-trot" log home, this Beaver Log Home features a breezeway between the house proper and the garage.

Ward Cabin Company's Laurentide log home, shows a traditional cabin design. Ample space for family living, plus, all the benefits of living in a forest atmosphere.

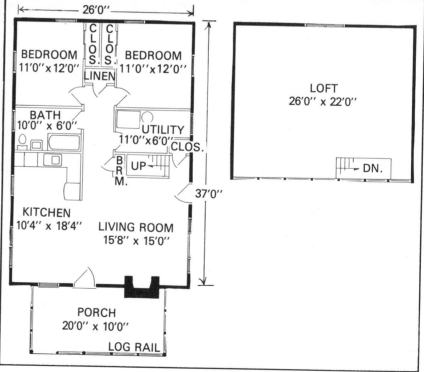

26'0"

BEDROOM
11'0" x 12'0"

CLOS.
CLOS.
LINEN

BEDROOM
11'0"x12'0"

BATH
10'0" x 6'0"

UTILITY
11'0"x6'0"
CLOS.

B
R
M.

UP

KITCHEN
10'4" x 18'4"

LIVING ROOM
15'8" x 15'0"

37'0"

LOFT
26'0" x 22'0"

DN.

PORCH
20'0" x 10'0"

LOG RAIL

Most log home builders compromise somewhere between a total prebuilt job and a complete from-scratch project. Bob and Jane Viebrock hired logs cut and sawed for their new three-bedroom home, but did virtually all of the construction work themselves.

"The sawmill operator bought standing timber, cut the logs, sawed them flat on three sides and delivered them to the building site," says Bob Viebrock. "The cost of the logs was just under $1,000 (in 1974) and that provided the walls, siding and a good part of the insulation in the walls."

The Viebrocks, with some help from friends, built their home according to plans Bob drafted himself. Even with some outside help, elapsed time from the point the basement was dug until the family moved in was more than two years.

"It took a lot of time and hard work, but we got a lot more home for our money than with any other construction method I can think of," says Viebrock. "Besides, I'd always wanted to see if I could build a log home — now I know that I can."

We'll have more on how the Viebrocks went about building their home in Chapter 7.

Other builders order precut kits from log home companies and do some or all of the construction work themselves. This allows considerable savings, compared with hiring all work done, and takes much less time than starting with the raw logs.

"Many of our customers erect their buildings themselves," says Kendall Buck, customer services director, Ward Cabin Company, Houlton, Maine. "Ward log homes are precut and all materials are labeled. There's very little cutting to be done on the job. Any builder with modest carpentry skills can build his own home, with some additional labor to help place roof purlins and tie-beams."

Like several other log home companies, Ward provides precut kits at more than one level of completeness, and priced accordingly. For example, the complete construction package for Ward's 37-by-26 feet "Laurentide" cedar log home is priced at $22,490.00 (as of December 1, 1977). The Laurentide starter kit, with log walls, studs for bearing partitions, purlins and supports, tie beams, exterior doors and windows, is priced at $15,360.00. Neither price includes transportation or on-site construction.

The extra $7,000 spent for the complete kit buys Anderson Perma-Shield windows, cedar cross rails, eave trim, shutters, basement windows, decks and other options not included in the starter package. If the homeowner could buy or build these features locally at less cost, the savings could help pay for electrical, plumbing and other non-structural building supplies.

Economy-minded home builders consider more than initial construction costs, too. Maintenance, energy efficiency and upkeep costs of a home merit more and more emphasis. Properly designed and well-constructed log homes get good marks in these areas.

For example, the Detroit Testing Laboratory, Inc., compared the heat loss and energy consumption differences between log construction and conventional materials. Horizontal tongue-and-groove joined eight-inch-diameter cedar logs required six kilowatt hours of electricity to maintain a temperature of 72 degrees F for 24 hours, when the outside temperature averaged 25 degrees. The researchers measured the heat loss through the log wall at an average 825 BTU's per hour.

In comparison, the scientists measured the same features in a conventional 2-by-4 studded wall, with 3 1/2 inches of fiberglass insulation in the wall cavity, half-inch sheetrock inside and 5/8-inch plywood siding outside. This structure required 8.1 kilowatt hours of electricity to maintain a constant 72 degrees of temperature, and researchers estimated heat loss at 1,151 BTU's per hour.

In these trials, both the log structure and the conventionally framed building had identical floors and roofs, so that the only difference would be in the insulating qualities of the walls.

Other Advantages

The durability of well-built log structures can be witnessed all over the U.S. Some wood species are naturally more durable and resistant to insect and decay damage than others, but most North American trees are potential home logs, if the wood is sound and treated with preservatives—and not placed in direct contact with the soil.

The choice of building materials for log homes formerly was dictated by the tree species growing in an area. But today, Alabamans can build with northern white cedar from Maine and Pennsylvanians can build with white spruce from the Rocky Mountains, if they wish — thanks to modern transportation and national companies that manufacture logs into building kits.

Cedar is the first choice of many log home builders. Verlin Jones, of Hollister, Missouri, a custom log home builder who has constructed more than a hundred houses, notes that cedar is easy to work and dries to about 50 percent of its green weight within six months. One log home company, Boyne Falls Log Homes, of Boyne Falls, Michigan, sells precut logs of northern white cedar, and has such faith in the durability of the wood that they guarantee their homes for ten years against rotting, cracking and insect damage.

Northern white cedar logs are the building material used by many log home companies. This conventionally styled home was built by Boyne Falls Log Homes, and the company guarantees the wood against cracking, decay and insect damage.

Fire Resistance

By the nature of their construction, log walls are more fire resistant than framed walls. The solid wood has slower char penetration, and has no "chimney" spaces, as in a conventional wall. This feature has prompted some insurance companies to revise premium schedules in favor of log homes.

Some Disadvantages

There are a couple of possible drawbacks to building with logs, however. In some areas, home mortgage lenders who view anything built of logs as a "cabin" may not be willing to loan on the basis of the completed home's true value. Also, not all prospective home buyers *want* to live in log homes—although more families are choosing log buildings all the time — which reduces the potential purchasers by some degree.

But most builders who have chosen to build with logs will already have thought past these stumbling blocks. A homeowner has his own priorities of reasons for building with logs in this day and age.

Growing Demand

Whether the motive is economy, appearance, nostalgia, durability or some combination of these, the log home is in great and growing demand among home builders. If a pioneer log-cabin builder were to appear on the scene today, he no doubt would be surprised at the popularity of this architectural throwback.

The choice to build with logs is not necessarily a statement about an owner's relative prosperity today. A log home may be a relatively inexpensive 500-square-foot A-frame, or enclose 4,000 square feet or more of floor space, with a total building ticket of well over $100,000.

2.

WHICH WAY TO GO— KIT, FROM-SCRATCH OR RENOVATE?

Regardless of where you live or the kind of house you plan to build, a good many decisions are made for you before you even get around to designing your home. The region of the country will to some extent influence the house you build, as will your budget, local building codes, style of living, etc.

Whether you create a log home from a prefab factory kit, from logs you cut locally (or hire cut) or from an existing older building will also depend upon existing factors. You may not have all these options from which to choose. You may have a source of logs, but lack the time, skill and labor to cut, handle and shape them into a livable house. You may have the time and skill to build a log home outright, but find that logs are not readily available.

You may own an older log building — house, barn or other structure — but find that the logs are too badly deteriorated to justify recycling into a modern home.

Each part of the country, and each home-building situation, presents a different set of problems to be solved. Each method of log home construction — from kits to building outright to remodeling or rebuilding an existing structure — offers benefits and disadvantages. The builder, as the saying goes, "pays his money and takes his choice."

However, it is better to make as many choices as you can *before* you pay your money. Here are some things to keep in mind.

Building From Kits

One big drawback to building a from-scratch log home is finding the logs. The woods are full of trees, of course, but unlike the days of Daniel Boone, most of those trees belong to someone else — often to someone who does not want them cut. Even if you own the trees, converting standing timber into a satisfactory home requires time, muscle and know-how.

For some builders, prefab or precut kits may be the best choice even if a source of logs is available. This is particularly true for builders whose time and labor are limited.

Many companies around the country sell milled logs, either in complete building packages or on a "per-log" basis. Most of the kit companies offer several design options; many employ draftsmen who will draw up blueprints from an owner's sketches.

A family can have its home designed, cut into a kit, shipped to the building site and erected, while a do-it-yourself home builder is still in the woods cutting logs.

"Delivery time for our company varies with the season," says Kendall Buck, of Ward Cabin Company. "However, three to four weeks after plans are approved is the usual time required to manufacture a custom-designed building."

By the way, the term "prefab" (from prefabrication) does not in any way describe the quality of either the design or the structure of a building. Prefab relates to the building process; the application of factory mass-production techniques to building materials. In fact, prefabricated and precut homes — both of frame and log construction — may often be of better quality than those built by conventional methods.

The packaged log home industry is growing rapidly, starting in Maine in 1931. A young lumberman named Bruce Ward started building cedar cabins, gradually refining techniques. He developed milling equipment to route a tight tongue-and-groove fitting on the facing surfaces of logs, and in the process built the leading log home company in the country.

Today, the log home business has spread all over, reflecting the growing acceptance of factory-cut-and-assembled log structures.

The convenience and time-saving of factory-milled logs has a price. The cost of a precut or prefab log building will depend on the location and the builder. Delivery charges typically run a dollar to $1.30 per loaded mile, from factory to the building site.

There is also some price variance with species of the wood and the amount of prefabrication done at the factory. In general, a completed kit-built log home will cost slightly more than a conventional wood frame building of equal quality and specifications.

"Our costs vary with the construction option you choose," explains Jack Copeland, president of Tall Timber Log and Construction Company, Boonville, Missouri. "We don't offer a kit, as such, because most builders want a home designed to their own specifications. We produce milled six-inch-thick tongue-and-grooved cedar logs. We'll deliver logs to the building sit for about $45 per lineal foot of wall" (in effect December 1977).

Tall Timber delivers logs free within 250 miles of the factory, and charges one dollar per mile for over 250 miles.

"We also have construction crews to provide about any level of building help the owner may need," says Copeland. "We'll construct walls on your foundations, rough in doors, windows and other wall openings for about $60 per lineal foot of wall. Or, we'll completely rough-in the shell, constructed with cedar shake roof, for about $20 per square foot of floor space."

Other companies offer different options. For example, Wilderness Log Homes, Inc., Plymouth, Wisconsin, offers a "full-log" kit of either 5 1/2 or eight-inch diameter logs. The company also builds an alternate "half-log" kit of frame construction with full-log corners, at a slightly lower price. The "half-log" package allows six inches of insulation to be placed in the wall cavity, and the interior walls to be finished with conventional dry-wall materials.

Wilderness Log Homes' "Hartland" model, a 35-by-25 1/2-foot, two-bedroom structure, sells for $11,802 (as of January, 1978) for the full-log complete

Packaged log homes can be had in all styles and sizes. Most log home companies offer custom designing services, to build homes to the owner's specifications (Courtesy Boyne Falls Log Homes)

package. The same floor plan, in the half-log-with-full-corners model is priced at $11,231. Neither price includes transportation, foundation or construction work at the building site.

The usual procedure for ordering a precut or prefab log home is to first contact the company or one of its dealers. (You'll find a listing of log home companies in Chapter 8.) In most cases the dealer or company representative can give you valuable help in designing a home to suit your family's needs or can help you select a standard plan that will be suitable, perhaps with some modification.

Once the plan is to your specifications, the next step is a purchase order the company will complete for your signature. This is a binding agreement, and most companies require a "good faith" deposit when the purchase order is signed. Twenty-five percent of the total package price appears to be the customary figure with most log home manufacturers. The balance of the payment is due when materials are delivered.

We'll have more on building log homes from kits in Chapter 8.

Build From Scratch?

Anyone with a reasonable amount of carpentry skill and standing timber can build a comfortable, durable log home. After all, our pioneer ancestors proved it over and over again as they spread west across North America. And if you have a source of logs, building a log home from the ground up can save a great deal of money compared with buying a kit or hiring professional construction labor.

Log construction has definitely moved beyond the "cabin" category. This 4,000-square-foot-plus home is being constructed of logs milled by Beaver Log Homes, Inc., Claremore, Oklahoma.

However, if you are building a log house from raw logs, be prepared for a lot of hard work. Working with heavy logs requires sweat as well as savvy, even if you use mechanical equipment to place the logs in position. Professional carpenters have been known to back off when it comes to building with whole logs.

The above paragraph is not intended to scare anyone out of the notion of building his home from the ground up, but to prevent any unpleasant surprises on down the line. If you start a log home project fully aware of the time and work involved, you are less likely to be discouraged if the work doesn't progress as quickly or smoothly as you had expected.

To build a log home from scratch, one that has your personal mark at each stage of the construction, you will need logs, time and some talent, but you are trading your labor and ingenuity for a home that is uniquely your own.

Next to a source of timber and the will to build your own home, what you will need most is *time,* particularly if you start with standing timber. The actual building of a log house need not take a great deal of time, but green logs should ideally be seasoned for six months. A year of air-drying is even better. Although green logs can be laid up directly — and many builders do this — extra care needs to be taken in building with unseasoned

Lots of open area characterizes the log home built by Clifford and Esther Hales. The Hales took advantage of areas behind roof eaves for additional storage. Note that the Hales left bark on the 8-inch logs in the house walls.

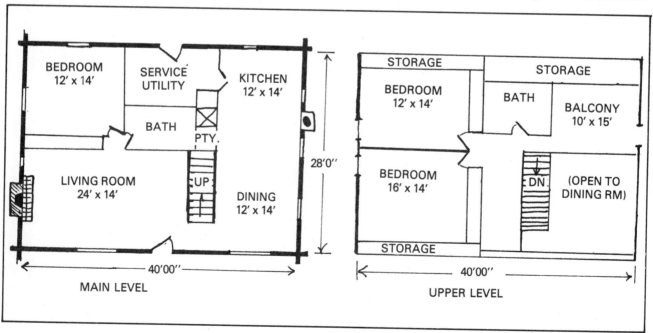

MAIN LEVEL

BEDROOM 12' x 14'

SERVICE UTILITY

KITCHEN 12' x 14'

BATH

PTY.

UP

LIVING ROOM 24' x 14'

DINING 12' x 14'

28'0''

40'00''

UPPER LEVEL

STORAGE

STORAGE

BEDROOM 12' x 14'

BATH

BALCONY 10' x 15'

BEDROOM 16' x 14'

DN

(OPEN TO DINING RM)

STORAGE

40'00''

Recycled log homes are the answer for some owners. Framed wings were added to this small log cabin, and the building materials of the framed ends were themselves recycled—the screened doors came from a dismantled grocery store nearby.

wood to allow for cracking, shrinking and warping as the logs dry in place.

Many builders prefer to use logs that have been sawed flat on three sides to standard dimensions. They either hire a sawmill to saw out their own logs, or buy logs sawed to specifications.

Success Story

Clifford and Esther Hales built their two-story home of purchased oak logs, sawed flat on three sides to a uniform eight-inch thickness. Hales left the bark on the rounded outer side of the logs.

The Hales' began construction in November, 1976, using a farm tractor and boom to lift the logs into position. Hales carefully built door and window frames as the walls went up. The family moved into the house ten weeks after the first log was placed on the foundation, although much of the interior of the house was still unfinished.

"A chainsaw is a most necessary tool in building a log home," observes Hales. "We did all the work, except milling the logs, pouring the foundation and building the fireplace."

Hales has not made a cost comparison between his three-bedroom, two-bath log home and a similar house of more conventional construction, but believes that he saved enough to earn a fair return on the time and labor he spent building the house.

Perhaps more to the point is Mrs. Hales' observation: "For years, we have wanted to live in a log home," she says. "This house is exactly what we had in mind."

It's that kind of return in satisfaction that lets the "from-scratch" log home builder know that his work and time were well worthwhile. We will explore building with locally procured logs more thoroughly in Chapters 6 and 7.

Recycle An Older Log Building?

Bill Kuykendall, a free-lance photojournalist of Keyser, West Virginia, is building a home of chestnut logs salvaged from a dismantled barn. Some of the squared logs are sixty feet long.

As the sturdy old barn came down, Kuykendall numbered each log. The logs then were hauled several miles to his building site, to wait until the builder had designed a home that accommodated both his own lifestyle and the character of his building material.

Kuykendall is doubly fortunate in his find. In the first place, older log buildings that are still sound enough to be remodeled or rebuilt are rare. Rarer still are log buildings made of chestnut. That species once dominated the forests in the eastern third of the United States, but it has long since fallen victim to a blight.

If you are lucky enough to find a patch of land with a sturdy, well-preserved log building on it, you will probably hope to remodel the structure, rather than build anew.

One drawback to older log cabins is their size; they are usually smaller than most families require. This can partly be overcome by clustering or combining two or more cabins if they are available, or by adding on to the existing cabin. Even then log cabins built years ago may not lend themselves to modernizing as they stand. Even if the space is adequate, rooms are not always arranged to suit modern living. Often, the best course of action is to dismantle and rebuild, even if the cabin need not be relocated to a different site.

Home builders prove to be an ingenious breed. If the material is available, the uses it can be put to are limited only by the builder's imagination and skill. Comfortable, attractive log homes have been built from recycled utility poles, bridge timbers and railroad crossties.

You will find more on building with recycled logs in Chapter 9.

Whichever route you choose, spend a good chunk of time in planning your home. There is a great deal of "prebuilding" to be done, before construction is started. This planning stage can help you head off serious problems later on. Give yourself plenty of time to create a design that suits the way you live.

3.

WHERE WILL YOU LIVE?

Most of us are sheltered by not one but several homes in a lifetime. We move from job to job, from city to city, from city to country, from country to city — with choices to make each time about the house we will occupy.

Where you locate your home will, oftentimes, be as important as the kind of house you build. Even if your new home will be occupied by your family for only a brief time, the house, the grounds and the neighborhood will affect your happiness and well-being for the time you live there. You may plan a house that is to be your home from now on, but when locating and designing the house give some thought as to its appeal for other home buyers — just in case still another move is in the offing some time in the future.

In your planning, start with the general and work toward specifics. Your geographical region should influence what, how and when you build.

In northern states and mountainous areas, winters are cold and snowfall is heavy. In the warm, humid southeastern U.S., wood decay and insect damage can be problems. In hot climates, venting and cooling summer air may demand more energy than winter heating. In regions with cold, damp winters, keeping warm and controlling moisture inside the house present difficulties. Deserts, ocean fronts, river valleys and hilltops all present their own unique delights and dilemmas to home builders.

You will want to study the climate of your region and incorporate the knowledge gained into the home

Frost Dates

State	Last in Spring	First in Fall	State	Last in Spring	First in Fall	State	Last in Spring	First in Fall
Alabama, N. W.	Mar. 25	Oct. 30	Iowa, So.	Apr. 15	Oct.9	N. Dakota, W.	May 21	Sept. 13
Alabama, S. E.	Mar. 8	Nov. 15	Kansas	Apr. 20	Oct. 15	N. Dakota, E.	May 16	Sept. 20
Arizona, No.	Apr. 23	Oct. 19	Kentucky	Apr. 15	Oct. 20	Ohio, No.	May 6	Oct. 15
Arizona, So.	Mar. 1	Dec. 1	Louisiana, No.	Mar. 13	Nov. 10	Ohio, So.	Apr. 20	Oct. 20
Arkansas, No.	Apr. 7	Oct. 23	Louisiana, So.	Feb. 20	Nov. 20	Oklahoma	Apr. 2	Nov. 2
Arkansas, So.	Mar. 25	Nov. 3	Maine	May 25	Sept. 25	Oregon, W.	Apr. 17	Oct. 25
California			Maryland	Apr. 19	Oct. 20	Oregon, E.	June 4	Sept. 22
Imperial Valley	Jan. 25	Dec. 15	Massachusetts	Apr. 25	Oct. 25	Pennsylvania, W.	Apr. 20	Oct. 10
Interior Valley	Mar. 1	Nov. 15	Michigan, Upper Pen.	May 25	Sept. 15	Pennsylvania, Cen.	May 1	Oct. 15
Southern Coast	Jan. 15	Dec. 15	Michigan, No.	May 17	Sept. 25	Pennsylvania, E.	Apr. 17	Oct. 15
Central coast	Feb. 25	Dec. 1	Michigan, So.	May 10	Oct. 8	Rhode Island	Apr. 25	Oct. 25
Mountain Slections	Apr. 25	Sept. 1	Minnesota, No.	May 25	Sept. 15	S. Carolina, N. W.	Apr. 1	Nov. 8
Colorado, West	May 25	Sept. 18	Minnesota, So.	May 11	Oct. 1	S. Carolina, S. E.	Mar. 15	Nov. 15
Colorado, N. E.	May 11	Sept. 27	Mississippi, No.	Mar. 23	Oct. 30	S. Dakota	May 15	Sept. 25
Colorado, S. E.	May 1	Oct. 15	Mississippi, So.	Mar. 15	Nov. 15	Tenneesee	Apr. 10	Oct. 25
Connecticut	Apr. 25	Oct. 20	Missouri	Apr. 20	Oct. 20	Texas, N. W.	Apr. 15	Nov. 1
Delaware	Apr. 15	Oct. 25	Montana	May 21	Sept. 22	Texas, N. E.	Mar. 21	Nov. 10
District of Columbia	Apr. 11	Oct. 23	Nebraska, W.	May 11	Oct. 4	Texas, So.	Feb. 10	Dec. 15
Florida, No.	Feb. 25	Dec. 5	Nebraska, E.	Apr. 15	Oct. 15	Utah	Apr. 26	Oct. 19
Florida, Cen.	Feb. 11	Dec. 28	Nevada, W.	May 19	Sept. 22	Vermont	May 23	Sept. 25
Florida, S. of Lake			Nevada, E.	June 1	Sept. 14	Virginia, No.	Apr. 15	Oct. 25
Okeechobee, almost			New Hampshire	May 23	Sept. 25	Virginia, So.	Apr. 10	Oct. 30
frost-free			New Jersey	Apr. 20	Oct. 25	Washington, W.	Apr. 10	Nov. 15
Georgia, No.	Apr. 1	Nov. 1	New Mexico, No.	Apr. 23	Oct. 17	Washington, E.	May 15	Oct. 1
Georgia, So.	Mar. 15	Nov. 15	New Mexico, So.	Apr. 1	Nov. 1	W. Virginia, W.	May 1	Oct. 15
Idaho	May 21	Sept. 22	New York, W.	May 10	Oct.8	W. Virginia, E.	May 15	Oct. 1
Illinois, No.	May 1	Oct. 8	New York, E.	May 1	Oct. 15	Wisconsin, No.	May 17	Sept. 25
Illinois, So.	Apr. 15	Oct. 20	New York, No.	May 15	Oct. 1	Wisconsin, So.	May 1	Oct. 10
Indiana, No.	May 1	Oct. 8	N. Carolina, W.	Apr. 15	Oct. 25	Wyoming, W.	June 20	Aug. 20
Indiana, So.	Apr. 15	Oct. 20	N. Carolina, E.	Apr. 8	Nov. 1	Wyoming, E.	May 21	Sept. 20
Iowa, No.	May 1	Oct. 2						

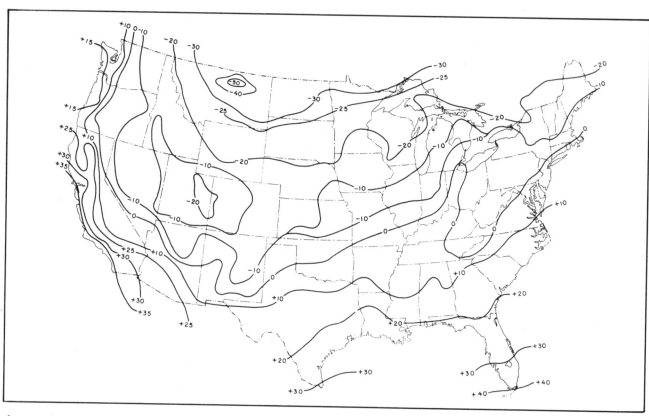

Average low temperatures in winter can help guide builders in selecting home-heating equipment and insulation for walls, ceilings and floors. Map is based on USDA Forest Service figures.

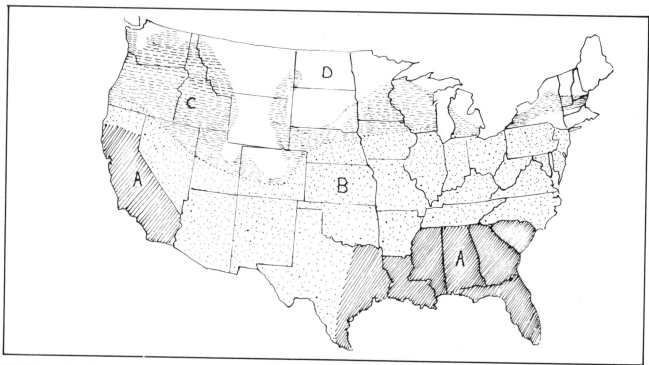

TERMITE SUSCEPTIBILITY BY GEOGRAPHIC AREA (a) Region I (including Hawaii): termite protection required in all areas. (b) Region II; termite protection generally required, although specific areas are sometimes exempted. (c) Region III: termite protection usually not required, except specific local areas that have been found hazardous. (d) Region IV (including Alaska): termite protection not required. SOURCE: U.S. Department of Housing and Urban Development (HUD) Minimum Property Standards. Washington, D.C.: Government Printing Office.

plan you choose or design. Check on annual average precipitation, mean temperatures for winter and summer, average days of sunshine in winter, especially if you plan to use solar heating.

The more you know about where you live, the better equipped you are to design and build a home that fits the area. For example, where snowfall is heavy, roofs need to be designed to carry the load. Salt air along the sea front can corrode metal; protection or alternatives must be considered. Heavy rains that would erode and mottle exterior finishes may mean that you will get along better if you let logs weather naturally.

Not only climate but other physical features of your region can affect your planning. In some areas of New England, for example, granite just under the soil's surface can push the price of excavation to half the total cost of a house. In the hills around Oakland and San Francisco, some soils are too unstable for safe building. In southern California, frequent droughts make fires a real hazard. River valleys and mud hillsides are subject to floods and mudslides; mountain tops are exposed to ceaseless wind; clay underfootings can shrink and expand with changing moisture content.

Wood decay caused by moisture and rain seepage is more of a hazard in some areas of the country than in others. Exposed building parts in the high-humidity area of the southeastern U.S. — logs, posts, porch and deck joists, flooring and rails, steps, roof fascia and molding—should be pressure-treated with preservative, unless a wood of high natural resistance to decay is used. In the "moderate" zones, a nonpressure treatment should be adequate. In "low" hazard areas, no treatment is needed.

Often, the topography of a region will vary widely, just within a few miles. For instance, the author's hometown in south-central Missouri sits on the dividing line between two distinct geologic areas. To the south and east, the land folds into the steep wooded hills and valleys of the northwestern Ozarks. To the north and west, rolling prairie land with deeper soils but fewer trees presents a totally different landscape.

The scenery is better in the hilly part of the county, but the rocky terrain creates excavation and landscaping headaches. In the prairie region, the deep loamy soil is more suitable for crops, gardens and pastures, but drainage can be a problem in flatter areas. Roads are harder to build in the hill country, but a drilled well there is likely to yield better water than in the prairie townships.

City or Country?

Where you live within a region may be dictated by your occupation, to some extent. If your job keeps you in town several hours each day, the cost of commuting to and from work — in time, money and fatigue — may outweigh the countryside benefits of space, privacy and quiet.

Wherever you decide to live, you will be concerned with local government policies on schools, fire and police protection, taxes, planning and zoning, as well as with such things as the cost of insurance and utilities. These and other social, economic and physical forces should be evaluated as you decide what kind of house to build and where you will build it.

In Town

If you choose to live in a town or city, hope to pick one that has an active comprehensive plan of zoning and growth. It is hard to predict the future growth of any city, but without an enforceable plan, expansion is likely to be less orderly.

Look over the neighborhoods within a community. Note their potential as development into commercial or industrial areas in the future. Do the zoning restrictions protect the residential area? Are stores, schools, churches and parks within a reasonable distance of the neighborhood?

Within the incorporated limits of cities and larger towns, check that services such as utilities, sewer, water, police and fire protection and street maintenance are available on a fairly standard basis. This is not always true of areas outside city limits.

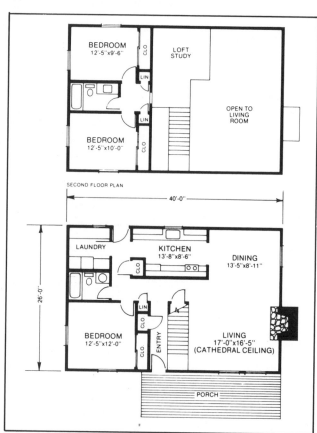

BEDROOM
12'-5"x9'-6"

LOFT
STUDY

OPEN TO
LIVING
ROOM

BEDROOM
12'-5"x10'-0"

SECOND FLOOR PLAN

40'-0"

LAUNDRY

KITCHEN
13'-8"x8'-6"

DINING
13'-5"x8'-11"

26'-0"

BEDROOM
12'-5"x12'-0"

ENTRY

LIVING
17'-0"x16'-5"
(CATHEDRAL CEILING)

PORCH

This story-and-a-half house utilizes a sill-and-post system of construction that allows walls to be preassembled in sections. The home is a standard Boyne Falls Log Homes design that features a cathederal ceiling over living room and dining room. (Photo courtesy of Boyne Falls Log Homes)

Ex-urban

For the past several years, the urge to move to the country, or at least to "outer suburbia", has been strong. People want to get away from the smog, dirt, crime and traffic of cities. They look for open spaces, trees, quiet, a place for a garden and room for a pony or two.

This trend is as prevalent around towns and small cities as in major metropolitan areas, and often creates brand-new problems for homeowners. Around urban centers, this movement out of town has resulted in a "hop-scotch" kind of residential development that combines the worst features of both city and country living. In smaller communities, with few or no restrictions or building codes, you may find expensive homes, cheap homes, mobile homes, service stations and beer joints all rubbing shoulders on the same block.

Evaluating Country Property

For some families, country living is ideal. They thrive on the space and privacy and vow never to move back to the city. People accustomed to the services and convenience of urban living, however, may have trouble adjusting to country life. Their responses may hinge on how well and how wisely each chose their country acreage.

What do you look for in a rural homesite? How do you evaluate the property once you have located it? You cannot automatically assume that services will be provided to the property. The cost of a road, water supply, electrical and telephone services and other necessities of modern living should be accurately estimated before buying the land. These are costs and judgments you will want to make before you sign any agreement to purchase a tract of land.

Do not take the realtor's word for it that the power company will string lines to your homesite free of any extra charge, or that a good deep well can be had for $300. It is not that real estate agents are dishonest, but their business is *selling* property. They are paid on a commission basis after the property is sold. Therefore, their objectivity in evaluating the property's value for you may be affected by their zeal to close the sale.

Buying property — in town or in the country — is similar to making any other capital investment. No investment is completely free of risk, but a decision based on facts properly evaluated can reduce the possibility of a bad investment.

The following property evaluation system is based on guides developed by agricultural economists at the University of Missouri. The purpose of this evaluation is

The cost of snow removal, and of any special equipment needed to maintain roads throughout the year, should be added to the selling price of any property isolated from hard-surfaced public roads.

not to place a dollar value on a piece of property, but to note features that affect it as a suitable homesite for your family.

Read through the entire scoring sheet on the following page before starting. Then, as you evaluate a potential property purchase, use scores of "0" through "4". Place a score of "0" on those features of the tract that are definitely undesirable. Assign a "4" to those attributes having superior qualities. Rank those features that are less than superior but not completely undesirable somewhere between "0" and "4". Remember, you are judging the property as it is now; not what it may be after improvements have been made. Mark your score in pencil so you can re-use it for alternative pieces of property.

Property Evaluation Sheet

Neighborhood

____Pleasing landscape
____Newer homes in area well maintained
____Direction and location relative to major
   trading center
____Acreage sizes of plots recently sold within
   your price range
____Any nuisances presently existing
   (noise, pollution, odors)
____Distance from city limits prevents annexation
   in forseeable future

Protection from adverse influence

____Property located in a flood plain
____Zoning laws in county
____Deed restrictions
____Property free of easements and incumbrances
____Property fenced (if needed or desired)

Services

____Road paved and well maintained.
____Adequate water supply
____Sewer or soil suitable for septic tank
____Utilities available: electricity, phone,
   gas, mail, etc.
____Reasonable cost for utilities
____Schools available and reasonable
   distance (bus route)
____Rural fire protection
____Churches
____Nearness to hospital and quality medical care
____Snow removal from adjacent roads
____Good routes to place(s) of employment

Costs

____Anticipated cost relative to living in urban area
____Real estate taxes
____Cost of property upkeep
____Transportation cost
____Special equipment or services needed
____Fire and liability insurance rates

Housing location

____Building site, in respect to total acreage
____Land well drained
____Trees
____Good exposure to sunlight
____Yard offers good potential for landscaping

TOTAL: _____

Notes:_____
_____
_____
_____
_____
_____
_____
_____
_____
_____
_____
_____
_____

An ever-renewable supply of heating fuel can be grown on a few acres of productive timberland. Figure that each acre will produce from one-half to one cord of wood each year, on a sustaining basis.

Once you have finished scoring the property, total the score and compare it with these suggested point groups:

- 100 points or more, the property is likely to be an excellent choice for your home site;

- 80 to 100 points indicates that the property may be a good choice, but look back over the scoring sheet to see which areas rank high, and which score low — a nearby school may be worth several points to a couple with small children, but be scored low by a retired couple;

- 65 to 80 points means the property is borderline, only fair as a potential homesite for your family — you may want to reevaluate the property or look for other tracts that score higher;

- 64 points or less, the tract is a poor choice, generally, so look around some more before buying.

Obviously, each prospective buyer will need to evaluate his own score sheet, and use his own scale as to which areas are more important. Some factors may affect the value of the property so much as to disqualify the tract. For instance, if the property is susceptible to flooding, this one undesirable feature could offset a straight "4" in all other areas.

Timber at the Site

As you will notice the evaluation system does not include a score for timber on the property, which may be an important feature for a builder who plans to cut his own logs. The fairest way to evaluate the trees on a wooded tract is to get an estimate of the value of the standing timber. State foresters with land-grant university extension services can help estimate the value of "on-the-stump" timber.

The value of timber as firewood should also be taken into account by homeowners who plan to partially or completely heat their homes with wood. You can use this general rule of thumb to estimate the firewood productivity of a wooded tract: with good timber management, an acre of hardwoods (oak, hickory, ash, etc.) should produce a cord of wood per year, almost indefinitely. (A cord is the measurement for 128 cubic feet of wood; or a stack four feet high, four feet wide and eight feet long.)

In your evaluation of property as a potential home site, you will want to consult with a lawyer and possibly other professionals before you make the investment. Some tracts of land are sold with limited ownership deeds; mineral rights or other ownership rights are held by another party. In some states, property owners cannot impound water on their land without special permission. Waste management regulations vary from state to state.

These special situations may not depreciate the property's value to you, but you should check into them before you buy.

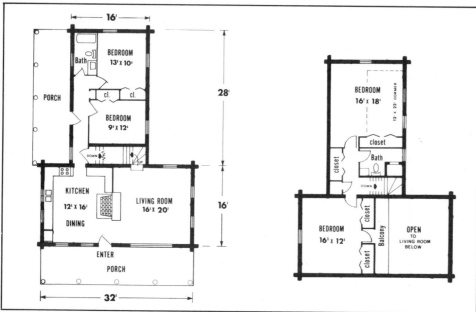

The Barrington model New England Log Home features 1,760 square feet on two levels, with a 22-foot dormer at the rear. The home shown in the photo is a modified version of the floor plan. (Courtesy New England Log Homes, Inc.)

4.

DESIGNING YOUR LOG HOME

Some builders start with a plan they particularly like, then look for a plot of land on which to build. To be sure you are able to build what you want, it is safest to determine first where you will build, then let the site influence what you will build.

Planning is the key ingredient to keep your dream house from becoming a nightmare. In Chapter 3 we talked about the importance of selecting the right setting for your home. You should also have found out about restrictions and building codes the ordinance-drafters have imposed on your portion of the good earth — square footage limits, setbacks, easements, sewage disposal rules and other things that will determine what and how you build.

In some regions with county zoning, for instance, one-family dwellings outside city limits can be built only on a minimum acreage — two, five, ten acres or some other arbitrary tract size.

Depending on the regulations, you may not be able to cut trees or impound water without a permit. More and more states and local governments are writing rules about sewage disposal, open burning and other activities that might affect the environment. Many of these features can influence your house design and construction.

After discovering the rules and restrictions, you will want to spend some time getting to know your land. Walk around it at different times of the day and night to get an idea of shade and sunlight patterns, and to see which view looks best at which hours of the day. One builder even spent two weeks camping on his 20-acre tract, pitching his tent first in one location, then

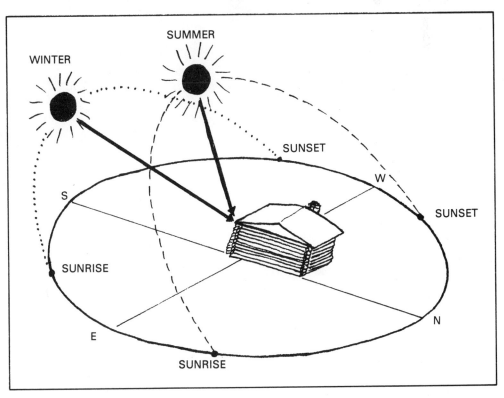

Position of the sun at noon, winter and summer, for about 40 degrees north latitude. Large glass areas to the south can take advantage of winter sun, which strikes the earth at a lower angle than summer sun. Glass should be double-paned to prevent heat loss in the winter.

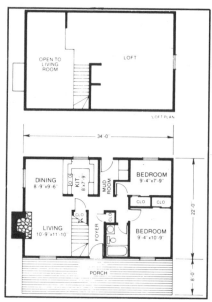

Traditional styling in this Boyne Falls "Centennial" home suits rustic settings. The manufacturer adapts the Centennial style to several different sizes and floor plans for stock precut kits. (Courtesy of Boyne Falls Log Homes, Inc.)

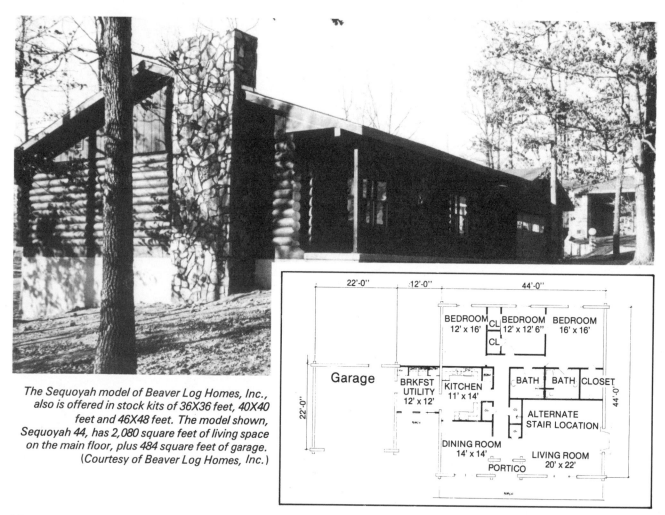

The Sequoyah model of Beaver Log Homes, Inc., also is offered in stock kits of 36X36 feet, 40X40 feet and 46X48 feet. The model shown, Sequoyah 44, has 2,080 square feet of living space on the main floor, plus 484 square feet of garage. (Courtesy of Beaver Log Homes, Inc.)

another, until he found the site that suited him best.

Make notes of the prevailing winds, the most scenic view, trees and shrubs to be retained or removed. Trees and other growth can shade summer sun or help shield the house from a winter gale's blast. But trees also can block out the sun when you would rather have it shining on an east or south window, and trees too close to the house can interfere with the sun and wind drying out log walls after a long wet spell.

If you value your privacy, do not build near your property line if there is a possibility that the land adjacent may be developed. And remember that deciduous trees can screen out sights and sounds in summer that may be all too apparent when the trees lose their leaves in winter.

By all means look at the soil your house will sit upon. Flooded basements and cracked foundation walls can be the result of ignoring peculiarities of the soil which is the basic foundation of your house. Talk to other builders, Soil Conservation Service specialists, and other experts if you have any doubt about how well the soil will support your house.

Once you know your land and have the "feel" of it, the next logical step is to choose a house design that suits both your purposes and building site. You may design your own home, hire an architect, order a plan through a stock plans service or use a log home company's standard plan — if you find one that fills the bill. Most plans services and log home manufacturers will make minor modifications to their standard plans.

Whatever route you choose, give a great deal of thought to how your family lives as you go through the planning process. What are your needs?

How many people are in your family? You may

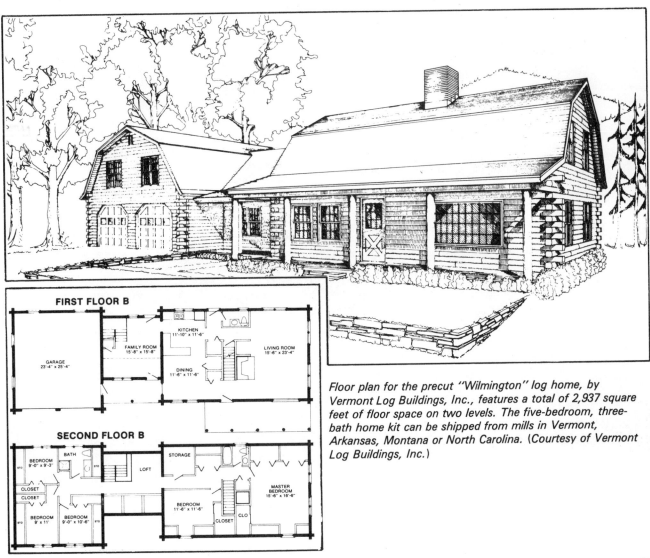

Floor plan for the precut "Wilmington" log home, by Vermont Log Buildings, Inc., features a total of 2,937 square feet of floor space on two levels. The five-bedroom, three-bath home kit can be shipped from mills in Vermont, Arkansas, Montana or North Carolina. (Courtesy of Vermont Log Buildings, Inc.)

need more storage space than most stock plans provide. A big family generates a lot of laundry, which may influence whether the utility room is located down a flight of steps in the basement or just off the kitchen.

How big is your building budget? A plan that "clusters" plumbing and other services helps cut down on building costs. Straight, uncomplicated lines in walls and roofs generally are less expensive to build than houses with many framing angles and roof levels.

Do you entertain often? You may want to consider your guests as you choose a layout for living room, dining room and kitchen.

Do you need an office or other workspace at home? Workshops are more convenient if located at ground level, with good access for deliveries. North light is best for painters' and artists' studios.

Do you frequently have overnight guests? Bedrooms are more pleasant on the quieter side of the house. Guests may feel more at ease if their bathroom adjoins the guest bedroom.

Does your family spend a lot of time outdoors? Maybe a good part of the living space can be provided with screened patios or porches.

How you intend to use your home will affect how you design it, inside and out. The following pages contain floor plans for several kit-built and from-scratch log homes. These are included merely as examples of what has been done with log construction. Hopefully, these designs will help stimulate your own planning. If, happily, you should find a design that suits perfectly, you are that much further along toward owning a log home that fits the needs of you and your family.

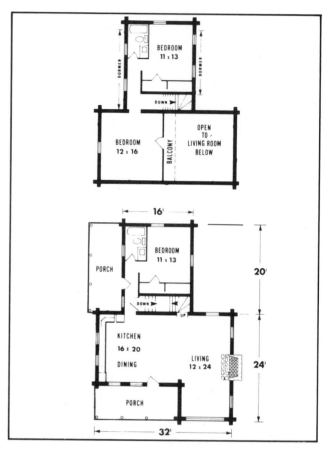

The New Englander design, by New England Log Homes, features 1,504 square feet of living space on two levels, plus two porches. The company provides blueprints and several hours of technical assistance with custom-plan kits. (Courtesy of New England Log Homes, Inc.)

Built from-scratch. Bob Viebrock's home of six-inch squared-on-three-sides logs features a steep roof line and double sliding glass doors that open onto a deck over the walk-out basement.

Clifford Hale's oak log two-story home is set off in winter by evergreens. Hales' home has porches front and rear running the full length of the house.

Mr. and Mrs. Richard Gerlt made full use of wood in their Boyne Falls log home—even to the seat for the toilet in the bathroom. The Gerlts selected prints and solid colors to complement the wood—in curtains, upholstered furniture, bedspreads, etc. (Courtesy Bill Mason)

A two-story fireplace can transform a ''log cabin'' into a rustic home. (Courtesy New England Log Homes)

Open log rafters and tie beams particularly suit log construction. Note the pole posts and handrail on the balcony. (Courtesy New England Log Homes, Inc.)

5.

EXCAVATION AND FOUNDATION

Early log homes often were constructed virtually without foundations; the logs were placed directly on the ground. Even where one or two courses of rough stones were used as a base to build on, little or no excavation was attempted.

The results are not hard to imagine. As the ground heaved and settled, as frost and ice worked on the building's underpinnings, the bottom logs and sills rotted. Floors began to sag and slope at angles other than horizontal. In a few years, the building was beyond use as a dwelling.

Today, most houses, of whatever materials, are built on a solid structure (usually masonry, but not always) anchored to the subsoil. The principal methods of supporting the weight of a house and its contents are (1) continuous foundation walls for basements or crawl spaces, (2) piers, or (3) concrete slabs poured on top of the ground.

Which method you choose will be determined by the size and style of building you construct, your budget, building codes in your area, and soil characteristics at the building site.

Whichever method you use, don't skimp on the foundation of your home. Just because the under-structure will be back-filled with dirt and be mostly out of sight is no reason to save pennies at this stage. If the foundation fails to support the house, it can mean spending big dollars later on. The slightest settling of the house platform can mean separated log joints, cracked interior walls, leaky roofs and jammed doors and windows.

In fact, you should think about building a heavier-than-standard foundation, because a house of solid logs weighs several tons more than one constructed with 2X4's on 16-inch centers. A few extra cubic yards of concrete and a few extra feet of reinforcing steel in the footing and foundation can be cheap insurance.

As we mentioned in Chapters 3 and 4, the conditions at your building site can influence the design of your home. For example, concrete slab foundations are best used on fairly level sites. On the other hand, a high ground water table may make a basement impractical, even on sloping sites. Your foundation should be designed specifically for the building it will support and for the site it will occupy.

Before you start digging, check the subsoil conditions by test borings to a depth equal to the foundation footing, or by inspecting existing houses built near your property. An experienced local builder can be worth a few dollars "consultant fee" even if you plan to do all the work yourself, and there's no better time to start consulting than at the beginning.

Locating the Walls

The first step in building, after the site has been cleared, is to mark the outside wall locations. If you are building a short foundation wall, piers or putting the building on a slab, you'll want to get corners exactly square to mark the perimeter of the house. If digging for a basement or deeper crawl-space foundation wall, you can be less precise about the location because you'll no doubt excavate a hole somewhat larger than the house foundation will be. You can pin down the exact perimeter after the excavation is made.

A level transit or other surveying equipment is handy, but not all that necessary. Here's a simple but precise way to do the job with a string, plumb bob and measuring tape:

First, establish a line where you want one wall of the house. Drive two stakes and stretch a line between them (Corners 1 and 2). The distance between the stakes should be the length of the wall on that side of the house. Drive tacks or small nails into the tops of these stakes to accurately mark the two corners established.

Now, if you remember the 3-4-5 principle of right triangles, the rest is easy. Measure along one end a

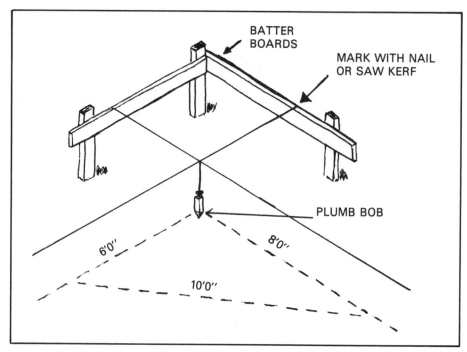

Squaring corners by the rule of 3, 4, 5.

BATTER BOARDS

MARK WITH NAIL OR SAW KERF

PLUMB BOB

6'0''

8'0''

10'0''

Method of laying out a building with batter boards and lines. The lines should mark the outside of the foundation.

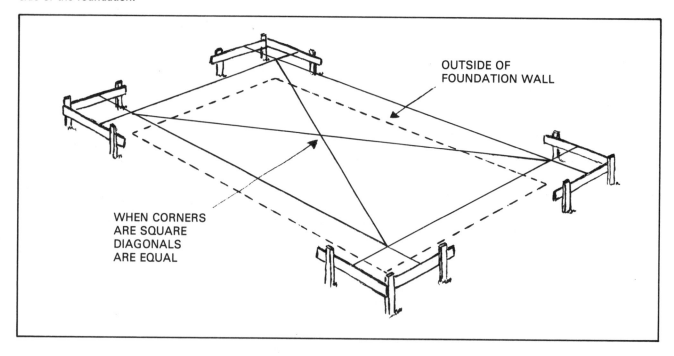

OUTSIDE OF FOUNDATION WALL

WHEN CORNERS ARE SQUARE DIAGONALS ARE EQUAL

distance in three-foot units (a multiple of three: i.e., 3 x 3 = 9) and measure along the adjacent side the same number of four-foot units (the same multiple times four; i.e., 4 x 3 = 12). The diagonal of these distances will equal the same number of five-foot units when the corner is an exact 90-degree angle (in this case, the diagonal would be three times five = 15).

Measure from one stake along the line you have established and drive a smaller stake exactly twelve feet from the corner. Now, measure off nine feet at a right angle from the same corner stake. After checking to see that the diagonal distance between the two stakes is exactly fifteen feet, drive a stake at this point. This gives you a square corner. You simply extend the nine-foot

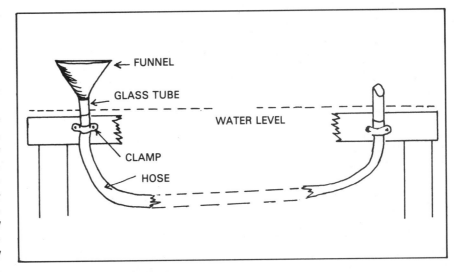

Use a water level to find height of foundation walls: Take hose with fittings removed, and two transparent tubes (one for each end); use plastic tape to make watertight joints between house and tubes. Insert funnel at one end and clamp this tube to batter board at "reference corner" (usually the batter board at the highest grade point). Take other end of hose to second corner and have someone slowly pour water into hose until water in first tube reaches exact height of first batter board. The water in the other tube should level out at precisely the same height; attach batter board at this height and repeat for last two corners.

line out to the required distance for the house wall to find the third corner. (You can use any multiples of 3, 4 and 5 to square corners.) To find the fourth corner of the building, repeat the procedure with the second corner you established on the original line. You can check the squareness of the layout by measuring the diagonal distances between opposite corners. These measurements should be equal. If your house is to be other than rectangular in shape, divide it into as many rectangles as necessary to square all corners. Round, hexagonal and octagonal buildings require different geometry for exactly straight lines, and you may want to get an engineer's help in layout of other than rectangular outlines.

After corners have been located and squared, drive three 2X4 stakes at each corner, three to four feet beyond the outside lines of the building. Nail 1X4 or 1X6 batter boards horizontally to these stakes at grade level, to mark the top of the foundation wall. Again, an engineer's level is handy for establishing the grade, but you can level the batter boards with a garden hose, as shown.

Fasten a stout string across the tops of opposite batter boards. Place the line over the tacks in the corner stakes, using a plumb bob to locate the line directly above the corners. Make quarter-inch saw cuts in the top of both boards at string locations, so the strings can be replaced later to mark the corners. You'll have to remove the corner stakes to excavate for the foundation, but the batter boards stay in place. Locate strings and saw cuts to mark each of the four walls.

When You Dig

Dig the general excavation only to the top of the footings, or to the bottom of the fill under the basement

Footings should rest on undisturbed soil. If footings must be placed in fill dirt, the dirt should be tamped well before footings are poured.

Some backhoe shovels are the proper width for foundation footings. If the excavation is made in stable soil, footings often can be poured without forming.

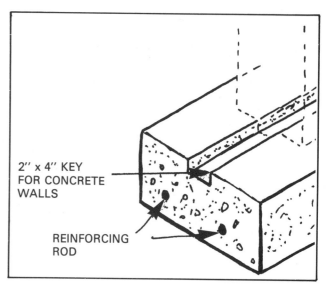

2" x 4" KEY FOR CONCRETE WALLS

REINFORCING ROD

Foundation footings should be at least twice as wide as the foundation wall is thick.

floor. A rain shower can soften some soils, and you want foundation footings on solid, undisturbed earth. So, carry out the final excavation for footings just before pouring the concrete.

A backhoe or power trencher can save a lot of time and digging. A bulldozer or tractor shovel can make quick work of excavating for a walk-out basement. Many backhoe shovels are 18 to 20 inches wide. If you hire an operator who knows his stuff, and dig the trench in stable soil that will stand pretty much vertically, you may be able to pour the concrete footing without any other form.

If you dig the excavation by hand, keep the trench sloped slightly to a low spot, so that water can collect and be pumped out of one place. Wet soil makes tough digging.

Deep excavations must be wide enough to work in when constructing and waterproofing the foundation or basement wall. Allow an extra couple of feet all the way around. How deep you will need to place the bottoms of footings depends on the depth of frost in your area and the type of soil you build on. Frost depth ranges from 12 inches or less in Gulf Coast states to six feet or more in New England. Generally, where footings of 48 inches or more deep are needed, basements are built.

Footings

Footings are the base of the foundation, and distribute the weight of the building over an area larger than the foundation itself. Footings also anchor the foundation to hold buildings in place.

The proper size of foundation footing will depend on the bearing value of the soil and the weight of the building. Generally, footings should be at least eight inches wider than the foundation walls. For log houses, poured concrete reinforced with half-inch steel rod is recommended for footings, whatever type of foundation is to be used. Reinforcing is particularly important at the corners of the footing to prevent cracking.

"We made the footings for our house 12 inches thick and a full 20 inches wide," says Clifford Hales, who built a two-story home from eight-inch-diameter oak logs. "The foundation-bed soil here is a gravelly clay, so we shouldn't have any settling or shifting."

If the footing width projects four inches or more beyond the foundation wall or pier, the footing thickness should be 1½ times the projection. In many areas, it is common practice to make the footing thickness equal to the thickness of the foundation wall. A footing 16 inches wide and eight inches thick is fairly standard for an eight-inch foundation wall. However, as noted earlier, with the extra weight of log houses, it is better to err on the side of strength. A 20-inch-wide footing under an eight-inch foundation wall would project six inches on either side of the foundation wall, and should be at least nine inches thick.

The same holds true for pier footings, which must bear the weight of their half of the beam or girder end of the joists. A 30-inch square footing under a 24-inch-square pier will extend six inches beyond the pier on all sides. The footing thickness should be at least nine inches.

Footings need to be bonded to the foundation. One way to do this with poured concrete walls is to use half-inch reinforcing rod cut to 10- or 12-inch lengths. When the foundation wall is poured, these rods are embedded one-half their length in the fresh concrete of the footing so they project into the foundation wall above the footing.

For foundations made of rubble stone, large stones can be set half their depth into the footing, about two feet apart. These stones then become part of the bottom row of stone in the foundation wall.

Continuous-Wall Foundations

Continuous-wall foundations that enclose basements or crawl spaces are the most satisfactory construction for buildings subjected to heavy loads. These foundations also make for warmer buildings, and are easier to pest- and rodent-proof than pier foundations.

Generally, foundations built of poured concrete are at least eight inches thick. Those built of precast concrete blocks or bricks should be the same minimum wall thickness. For log houses, rubble stone foundation walls should be 12 inches or more thick.

Poured concrete and concrete block foundation walls should be reinforced at corners and at the junction of other walls (porches, stoops, etc.). Bolts at least 5/8-inch in diameter should extend 12 inches or more into concrete foundation walls and 24 inches or more into unit-masonry walls (blocks, brick or stone). These bolts should extend above the top of the foundation wall far enough to bolt a sill, or the first course of logs, every eight feet around the perimeter of the foundation wall.

You *can* form up and pour a concrete foundation wall from cement mixed at the site. But the best

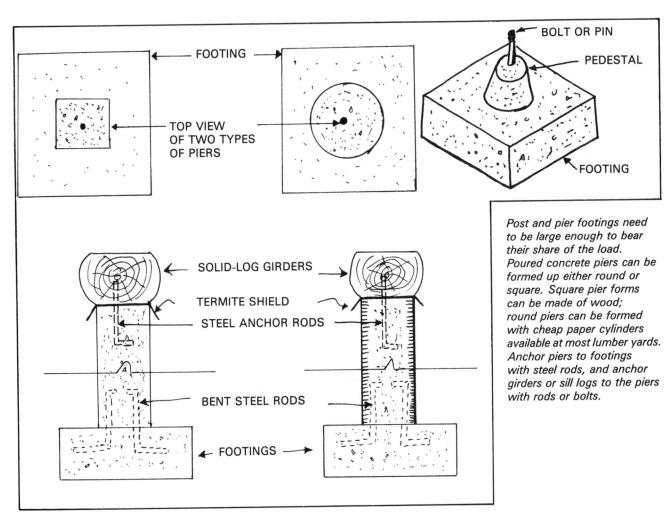

FOOTING

TOP VIEW OF TWO TYPES OF PIERS

BOLT OR PIN

PEDESTAL

FOOTING

SOLID-LOG GIRDERS

TERMITE SHIELD

STEEL ANCHOR RODS

BENT STEEL RODS

FOOTINGS

Post and pier footings need to be large enough to bear their share of the load. Poured concrete piers can be formed up either round or square. Square pier forms can be made of wood; round piers can be formed with cheap paper cylinders available at most lumber yards. Anchor piers to footings with steel rods, and anchor girders or sill logs to the piers with rods or bolts.

concrete construction is poured continuously — and quickly — without interruption from start to finish. You'll need several helpers to puddle and work the concrete in the form. That fact, plus the material wasted in building one-time-use forms makes pin-together re-useable forms and ready-mixed concrete among the better buys in construction.

In most areas, you can rent (maybe even borrow) metal forms for either foundations or basement walls. These forms fasten together with metal straps to make a rigid, even-width container for the wet cement. The time-consuming chores of cutting and fitting spacer blocks and wiring forms together are eliminated.

For foundations walls up to about three feet in height, you can build your own forms rather easily and without much material waste. The accompanying sketch shows how to build the footing so that bottom spacers in the foundation wall form are eliminated.

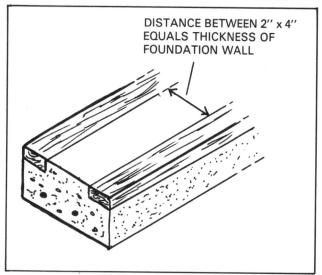

DISTANCE BETWEEN 2" x 4" EQUALS THICKNESS OF FOUNDATION WALL

Built-in spacers in the footing eliminate the need for the usual spreaders and lower braces when the foundation wall is formed later. Use reinforcing rod to pin the foundation to the footing.

Once the walls have been poured, the forms should stay up until the concrete has set enough to support itself and the initial weight that will be placed on it. That means at least two days when temperatures are above 50 degrees; (see frost chart, Chapter 14) as long as a week when the mercury hovers near the freezing mark.

After forms are knocked down, the foundation walls should be moisture-proofed. Waterproofing is particularly important for basement walls where several feet of soil will be back-filled against the wall.

Two coats of asphalt cement applied to the exterior of foundation walls will provide good waterproofing in most cases. Or, you can apply two coats of cement

mortar, each about 3/8-inch thick. Mix the mortar with one part Portland cement and three parts of clean, fine sand. Apply the mortar from the top of the footing to several inches above the final grade at the top of the foundation wall.

Concrete Slab Floors

Slab floors can be cast with the foundation, as one reinforced unit, or poured independently of the foundation — usually isolated from the foundation with a vapor barrier and two or more inches of rigid foam insulation. We'll discuss insulation further in Chapter 13.

In warmer climates, the integral slab-foundation method serves well. But solid concrete can conduct a lot of heat out of the house; in chillier regions, it is best to insulate the slab from the foundation.

The soil under a slab floor should be stable enough to prevent the concrete from cracking and settling. Over the leveled soil, distribute and level at least four inches of washed gravel or crushed rock. Over the rock, place a vapor barrier of plastic sheeting or 45-pound roofing felt, with overlapped joints. Then, put down reinforced steel mesh before pouring the four-inch-thick slab.

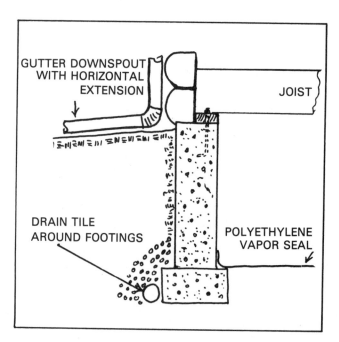

GUTTER DOWNSPOUT WITH HORIZONTAL EXTENSION

JOIST

DRAIN TILE AROUND FOOTINGS

POLYETHYLENE VAPOR SEAL

Drainage tile around footings, backfilled with two or three feet of coarse gravel, can help cure damp basements and crawl spaces.

Basement walls that are to be backfilled with dirt should be waterproofed. Builder here has used asphalt cement.

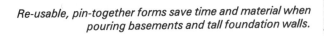

Re-usable, pin-together forms save time and material when pouring basements and tall foundation walls.

Continuous poured concrete foundation or basement walls are the best underpinnings to carry the weight of log houses. If stone or brick is desired for effect, the masonry can be laid up over the concrete, as in this basement wall.

Pier Foundations

The least expensive foundation is piers made of poured concrete, concrete blocks, brick, stone or wooden posts. In marshy or swampy areas, the best foundation may be pressure-treated wooden piles well driven.

Pier spacing depends largely on soil conditions and building weight. Concrete piers that are more than two feet high should be reinforced at corners with vertical steel rods that extend into the pier footing.

The bottom-most wooden members of the building (sills, plates or logs) should be bolted to piers, with bolts set 12 inches or more into the pier.

For warm floors in chilly weather, insulation can be installed between floor joists of buildings placed on piers. The space between outside piers also can be closed in with curtain walls, but this defeats much of the economy of using piers in the first place.

Unless there is some condition that dictates otherwise, a continuous-wall foundation is the best bet for a larger log house. And if possible the wall should be of poured concrete. A stone foundation helps set off the appearance of a log home, it's true. But you may want to pour a concrete foundation wall, then lay up or "veneer" rock over it for appearance.

If your building budget demands that you economize, try to do it somewhere other than in the footing and foundation. These members support the rest of the house, and they are darned expensive to repair or replace.

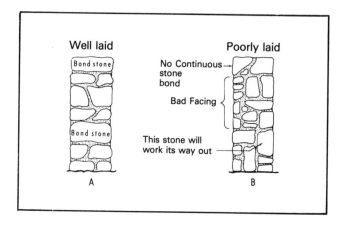

If stone foundation walls are used, the walls should be at least 12 inches thick and the stones well bonded. (Courtesy of USDA Forest Service)

Concrete slabs can be poured either integral with the footing, or all in one piece, in warmer climates where there is little frost heaving of the soil beneath (as in "A", below) For cooler regions, a continuous footing and foundation wall, as in "B", will be more satisfactory. In either type of construction, the slab should be poured over at least four inches of washed gravel or crushed rock, which is covered with a vapor barrier.

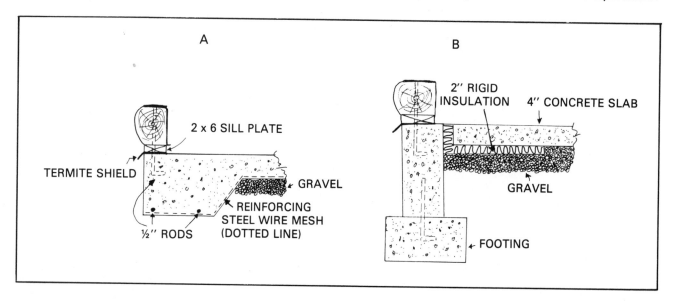

6.

CUT YOUR OWN LOGS?

Cost Comparisons

If you are lucky, you have logs on or near your property that can be cut for your home. You can harvest your own timber and hire the logs sawed flat on two or three sides for considerably less cash outlay than you would spend to buy the logs outright. Or, you can hew the logs flat — lay them up round, if you wish — and save even more money.

How much will purchased logs cost? A 30-by-40-foot house, with the normal number of wall openings, will require about 1,340 running feet (lineal feet) of 8-inch logs. In most areas of the country logs cost from $1.60 to more than $2 per lineal foot (as of January, 1978). That puts the cost of material for the walls at $2,000 to $2,500: this pays for someone else's timber, the labor to cut and haul the logs, and the mill work to get the logs sawed to a uniform thickness.

Milled logs with tongue-and-groove or splined joints will cost considerably more than that. Cost also will vary with the species of wood used. Timber with popular alternative uses — cedar, spruce, cypress, — will cost more than rougher woods that are in less demand for other purposes.

To compare buying logs that are already sawed to cutting your own timber and hiring a mill to saw the logs, figure it this way: 1,340 feet of eight-inch logs contains about 8,040 board feet of lumber. (A board foot is 144 cubic inches of wood, or equal to a piece of wood one inch thick and 12 inches square). At a sawmill rate of 12 cents per board foot, the bill for sawing out logs comes to about $965. Even with a trucking charge of several hundred dollars, the cost is still considerably shy of the $2,500 for buying logs.

Even if you don't have log-sized timber on your property, you may be able to cut your own. Often, logs can be cut from rights-of-way for new power lines, highways or other eminent domain construction. Farmers and other landowners may have a timbered acreage they want cleared for crops or pasture land.

Occasionally, you can find usable logs in "dozer piles" where timber has been cleared with a bull-dozer. It's worth checking out.

Choosing Wood

In this day and age, you are fortunate if you have available exactly what you want in the way of timber for logs. In general, softwoods (cedar, pine, spruce, fir) are lighter and easier to work than such hardwoods as oak or ash. Softwoods (depending on where and how they grow) also usually have less taper and fewer limbs on the lower trunk. So, if you have the choice between red cedar and red oak, build your house of cedar logs.

But for a practical matter, you will have to use whatever species is available. In fact, you may use more than one, even in the same wall. Virtually all woods can be used as house logs if they are handled and treated properly.

The species of logs you use and where you build your home may in part dictate details of the construction. For example, species of wood vary inherently in insulation value. Highest in insulative value are the softwoods, ranging from about 1.4 units of R-value (resistance to heat passage) per inch of thickness for northern white cedar to 0.95 R-value for southern yellow pine. By comparison, white ash ranks about 0.85 R-value, and white oak about 0.75. That means an eight-inch-thick piece of northern white cedar has an R-value of 11.2 (better than 3½ inches of fiberglas insulation), while eight inches of white oak measures only about R-6.

Happily, softwoods are more abundant in northern and mountainous regions, where more insulation is needed in winter; while hardwoods predominate in central and southern forests. It's almost as if Mother Nature had log home builders in mind when She stocked the forests.

R-value of a log wall can be increased by furring or studding the inside, adding a fiberglas or other insula-

Properties of Woods

Species	Strength	Weight	Working Ease	Decay Resistance	Shrink/ Cracking
Ash, white	high	heavy	hard	low	high
Beech	high	heavy	hard	low	high
Birch	high	heavy	hard	low	high
Cedar, red	medium	medium	easy	very high	low
Cedar, white	medium	medium	easy	very high	very low
Cottonwood	low	light	medium	low	med.-high
Cypress	medium	medium	medium	very high	low
Fir, Douglas	medium	medium	medium	medium	medium
Gum	medium	medium	medium	medium	medium
Hickory	high	heavy	hard	very low	high
Maple, hard	high	heavy	hard	low	high
Oak, red	high	heavy	hard	low	med.-high
Oak, white	high	heavy	hard	medium	med.-low
Pine eastern white	low	light	easy	medium	low
Pine, ponderosa	low	light	easy	low	med.-low
Pine, yellow	high	medium	medium	medium	med.-high
Spruce	low	light	medium	low	medium
Walnut, black	high	heavy	medium	high	medium

NOTE: Some woods that otherwise might be suitable for house logs may be priced out of practical use. Black walnut, for instance, is a strong, decay-resistant wood that is fairly easily worked: However, the price for veneer grade walnut can be several dollars per board foot—on the stump. A builder might get more milage out of this timber if he sold it for cash, then bought logs of other species for his house.

tion layer and finishing the walls with conventional drywall materials. While this may offend the aesthetic sensibilities of those who prefer log wall interiors, it can help cut down on energy bills and make a house more comfortable.

It also increases construction costs, of course.

Into the Woods

The first thing to determine is whether you have enough logs of the right kind and size to build the house you want to build. Before you gas up the chainsaw, you'll need to "cruise" the timber to select those trees that will produce suitable logs.

When choosing trees to be cut, keep in mind that you'll have to drag or skid them out of the woods. A prime log lying in the bottom of a steep ravine can require a lot of retrieval time.

Let's suppose you need 200 logs, of an average eight inches in diameter and an average of 12 feet in length. Professional foresters use several gadgets to measure the size and length of logs "on the stump," but you can do the same thing with a dressmaker's tape

measure and a straight stick about four feet long. You will also need something to mark the trees to be cut. A can of bright spray paint will do the trick. Or you can carry a small hand axe or hatchet to "blaze" a mark.

To estimate the diameter of a tree, hark back to grade school math. The diameter of a circle, you'll recall, equals the circumference divided by *Pi* (3.14). In other words, a log's diameter is approximately one-third of its circumference or distance around.

Measure the circumference at breast height, or four feet above the stump. If you are after an eight-inch peeled log, consider that the log is wrapped in a couple of inches of bark. So, the minimum circumference at breast height should be 32 inches.

Here's the way to compute it: eight inches of log, plus two inches of bark, equals 10 inches diameter. The distance around a circle with a 10-inch diameter is 31.4 inches (10 x 3.14). And, since the log will taper to something less than eight inches at a 12-foot height, the minimum circumference at breast height should be about 32 inches.

You'll probably want to set a maximum measurement to make sure the logs are reasonably uniform in thickness, particularly if the logs will be laid up round, or nearly so. Perhaps you will mark for cutting only logs that measure between 32 and 40 inches in circumference. If the logs will be sawed at a mill, the maximum measurement is not critical, since the logs can readily be sawed to a uniform width and thickness.

To estimate the length of log in a tree trunk, take a straight stick and measure along the stick exactly the distance from your "sighting eye" to your fist, with your arm extended horizontally. Mark on the stick a length equal to that distance. To use this homemade gauge, hold the stick vertically, with the mark just even with the top of your fist. The distance from your hand to the top of the stick should equal the distance from your hand to your eye. Back away from the tree, on relatively level ground, until the line of sight over your fist intersects the base of the tree and the line of sight over the top of

the stick intersects the top end of the usable trunk. As you sight, move only your eye — not your head. The distance from where you stand when the sight-lines intersect to the base of the tree will equal the tree's height.

Remember: you want to measure only the potential log in the tree, not the topmost branches.

While you are out there in the woods, measuring and selecting logs for your future home, make a note of skidding routes to be used later on. You'll have to get those logs out of the woods, and a little planning can save time and work on down the line. Try to pick trails through areas where only small trees and underbrush will need to be cut to open up a route. Larger trees take more time to work up and clear, and also leave big stumps that get in the way.

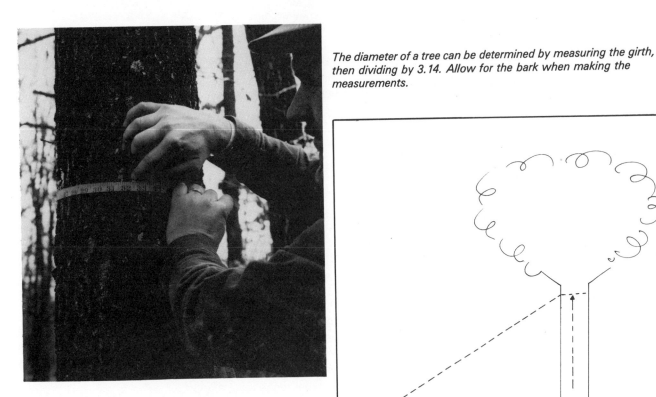

The diameter of a tree can be determined by measuring the girth, then dividing by 3.14. Allow for the bark when making the measurements.

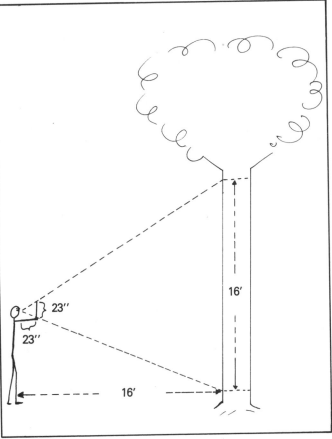

A straight stick, measured to the distance from eye to fist (example shown: 23") can be used to accurately estimate the length of a log in a standing tree.

Trees should be cut close to the ground, to get more usable log and to keep stumps low enough to prevent later interference with skidding logs.

Logs from trees sawed near the ground will have a bell-shaped bulge at the butt end. The log can either be bucked off above this bulge, or trimmed.

Tools You'll Need

You won't need a big investment in timber-working tools to cut logs for a house, but the tools you do select should be kept in good condition.

Remember that saws work best across the grain, at right angles to the trunk of the tree. Axes, for lopping limbs and clearing underbrush, cut best at an oblique angle. And wedges are used to split wood with the grain. Keep these functions in mind to help you select the implement that best suits the job to be done.

Despite its noise and smell, the chainsaw is an almost indispensable tool, particularly for one-man logging operations. Professional loggers have their own preferences as to models and sizes, but all chainsaws built by reputable manufacturers are serviceable machines. More important than brand name will be the level of service provided by the dealer who sells you the saw. Chainsaws, like all machines, need maintenance and repair from time to time — all types and all brands.

Don't make the mistake of buying too large a chainsaw. A 30-pound machine gets mighty heavy after a couple of hours' steady sawing. A lightweight, direct-drive saw with a 16- or 18-inch cutter bar will handle trees up to 30 inches in diameter and larger.

Cutter teeth on chains vary in size and bevel. To do their job properly, teeth require sharpening to just the right depth and angle. Chainsaw files are sized by diameter, and are made in sixteenth-inch size increments. Use a file of exactly the right size. A file holder and filing gauge help get a precise sharpening job without removing the chain from the saw.

The high-pitched snarl of a chainsaw engine has been labeled by the Occupational Safety and Health Administration as one of the noises that can damage hearing. You may want to use ear-plugs when operating the saw, or those high-level noise suppressors that filter out loud noises but still let you hear sounds in lower-decibel ranges.

Axes, like saws, depend on the preference of the wielder. Many timber men use a double-bit axe with a 3½ or 4-pound head. A single-bitted axe is somewhat safer to use, however you still have a 50-50 chance of banging your leg with the blunt side of the thing. If you haven't had much experience at chopping (enough to have developed a liking for a particular kind and weight of axe) try both kinds, then select the axe that suits you best. You'll probably also want a smaller hand-axe or broad-bladed hatchet for lighter chopping.

Timber working tools include, from the top clockwise: cant hook for rolling logs, chainsaw, one-man crosscut hand saw, ratchet winch, log chain, hammer and wedges for splitting wood, felling axe (some timbermen prefer a single-bit axe) and broadaxe for hewing logs.

Cutting tools must be sharp to do the job. Saw chain teeth must be filed at the correct angle and bevel, with a round file sized for the particular chain.

For cutting logs you will have little need for steel wedges, although they do come in handy for splitting big logs into firewood. When felling trees and bucking off logs, a wedge often is needed to hold the saw kerf open to prevent pinching the saw blade. However, wooden or hard rubber wedges serve this function as well as steel ones, and you won't have to spend the next 30 minutes filing a saw, should the chain happen to hit the wedge.

Other tools you may need include a cant hook or peavey to roll heavy logs. Both of these tools have a single tong (or "dog") at the end to grip the log, and a handle for leverage. The main difference is that the peavey is equipped with a steel spike on the end of the handle.

A ratchet hoist, or "come-along", is surprisingly useful for dislodging trees that are hung up on their neighbors. And, you will need a heavy chain to drag logs. Choose a chain that has a grab hook (a hook that will engage the chain links) on one end and an open or slip hook on the other.

Unless you develop more precision than most chainsaw operators muster, you will also need a saw to make square cuts on log ends. A bow saw or a one-man crosscut saw will do this job nicely.

Cutting Trees

There's a great argument over which is the best time to cut logs. Some say do it in winter, when sap is

Cutting the Tree

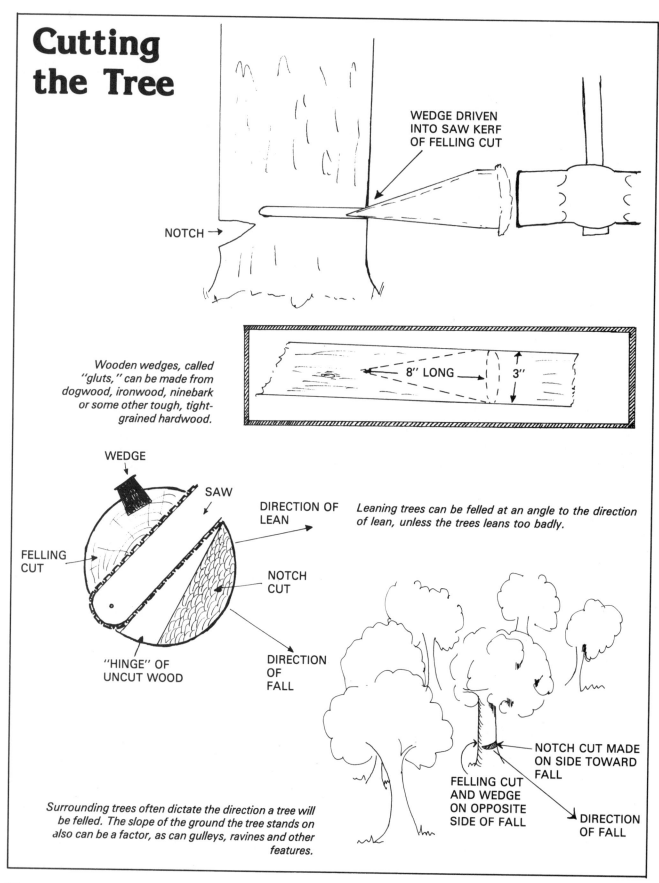

WEDGE DRIVEN INTO SAW KERF OF FELLING CUT

NOTCH →

Wooden wedges, called "gluts," can be made from dogwood, ironwood, ninebark or some other tough, tight-grained hardwood.

8" LONG

3"

WEDGE

SAW

DIRECTION OF LEAN

FELLING CUT

NOTCH CUT

"HINGE" OF UNCUT WOOD

DIRECTION OF FALL

Leaning trees can be felled at an angle to the direction of lean, unless the trees leans too badly.

NOTCH CUT MADE ON SIDE TOWARD FALL

FELLING CUT AND WEDGE ON OPPOSITE SIDE OF FALL

DIRECTION OF FALL

Surrounding trees often dictate the direction a tree will be felled. The slope of the ground the tree stands on also can be a factor, as can gulleys, ravines and other features.

down, because the logs will dry faster. Others say cut them in spring, when the sap is rising, because the logs will be easier to peel.

The most practical answer is probably to cut logs whenever you have the time and opportunity. Unless you have some help, or can work full time in the woods, your log-cutting probably will span more than one season of the year anyway.

Timber work can be dangerous, but it needn't be. It's bad form to whack a foot with an axe, of course. And no one intentionally stands in the way of several tons of trunk and branches as a tree crashes to the earth. These are such obvious hazards that warnings are hardly necessary.

However, most woodlot injuries are of more subtle origin: A dead limb breaks off just as the tree starts to fall; a sudden gust of wind deflects the tree from the planned direction of fall; a limb or bush trips the sawyer or axeman. A few seconds' time to notice and clear potential hazards make timber work a lot safer. Hurry is a poor partner to take into the woods.

The easiest and safest tree to drop is one that stands absolutely vertical, without heavy limbs that unbalance the tree in one direction. Such a tree can be felled accurately in any one of the 360 degrees around it.

The first step is to decide which way to fell the tree. Your choice probably will be dictated by other trees growing in the area. You will want to drop the tree where it will do the least damage to other trees, and where there is the least chance of the tree "hanging up" in another as it falls.

Clear the brush and dead limbs from around the trunk of the tree, and choose an escape route before you start sawing. As the tree starts to fall, you'll want to move back — 10 feet or more — at an angle away from the direction of fall. The fact that a tree sometimes splits at the stump or springs back when the branches hit the ground makes the area around the stump hazardous, particularly the area directly opposite the direction of fall.

Now, you are ready to make the notch, or under-cut. This notch is made to about a quarter of the tree's diameter, in the direction the tree is to fall. The notched-out section lets the tree start falling where it is supposed to fall. Make the first cut of the notch horizontal, with the plane of the saw blade parallel to the ground. Then, make a second cut downward at about a 45-degree angle to meet the inside edges of the horizontal cut. It takes a little practice to make the two cuts meet just right. But once you've got the hang of it, the wedge-shaped piece of wood will fall out of the notch.

To make the felling cut, start on the side of the tree opposite from the notch. Make a cut that is horizontal and about two inches above the base of the notch already cut. Saw directly through the tree to within about two inches of the notch. The wood that is left between the two cuts acts as a hinge that controls the direction of fall.

Don't saw the tree completely through; a sudden gust of wind could send it crashing in any direction. As the felling cut slices to within a couple of inches of the notch, start a wooden or hard rubber wedge in the saw kerf opposite the notch. Give the wedge a couple of taps with the hammer to pry the tree slightly in the direction you want it to fall. This also prevents the tree from rocking back and pinching the saw.

As the tree starts to fall, the felling cut will widen: slowly at first, then more rapidly as gravity pulls on the tipping tree. Stop sawing and remove the saw. If the tree doesn't fall right away, drive the wedge in to force the tree over.

Problem Trees

Trees that lean and those with a lop-sided weight of limbs mean trouble. The simplest solution is to drop the tree in the direction it leans. You'll want to watch a "leaner" closely, however. The weight of the leaning tree will make it fall sooner — and fall faster — than a tree that stands more nearly vertical. The tree usually starts to fall before the "hinge" of wood between the notch and felling cuts is narrow enough to be effective. Because more uncut wood remains, the trunk of a leaning tree often splits and splinters as the tree falls.

If a tree does not lean too badly it can be felled somewhat to one side or the other of the direction of lean. Suppose you want to cut a tree that leans into a second tree; the problem is that the tree you are cutting may become lodged in the second tree if it falls in the direction it leans. Here's how to "pull" the tree to one side.

Make the notch in the direction you wish the tree to fall, but only slightly to the side of the leaning direction. Then, when the felling cut is made, cut through nearly to the notch on the leaning side of the tree, but leave more "hinge" wood on the other side, to hold and swing the tree to fall where you want it. A wedge driven into the saw kerf opposite the notch also helps.

The wind can help or hinder your efforts to drop a tree where you want it. A steady breeze can be compensated for, but you'd better sit out those days when winds are strong or gusty.

All of this takes much longer to explain than to do, of course. You probably will cut your first tree only after much study and planning. By the fortieth or fiftieth, you'll automatically note which way and how much the tree leans, the best spot for it to fall, and where to start cutting the notch — all in a matter of seconds. As the felling cut nears the notch, you'll know when to watch for that first slight widening of the saw kerf that tells you the tree is tipping off balance. You'll already have decided which way to retreat as the tree falls. Timber work, as any other skill, takes experience and judgment that come only with practice.

De-Limbing Logs

Once trees are on the ground, you must lop off limbs and saw off the logs. How you go about this depends on your preference, and how much time you have at each working stint in the woods.

If you can work several days in a row, you may want to saw down a number of trees, then go back later to work them up into logs. However, if you have only a few hours to work at a time, you may prefer to saw down a tree, lop off limbs, buck off the log, then go on to the next tree. With a helper, both operations can be going on at the same time.

Some woodsmen use their chainsaw to cut limbs, rather than try to keep up with an axe. They fell a tree, then move right up the trunk, sawing off limbs flush with the stem of the tree. When they have trimmed the length of the log they want, they saw downwards about three-fourths of the way through the trunk. Then, if the trunk is supported off the ground by limbs and branches, they move the saw blade under the log and make a cut upward to meet the first cut. (Be careful when cutting with the top edge of a chainsaw blade. The chain's direction of travel tends to push the saw out of the wood, and can cause the saw to kick back.)

If the trunk is lying flat on the ground, you can use a pole to pry it up, put a chunk under it and finish sawing off the log. This technique takes some practice to master, and involves the occasional frustration of sawing too nearly through the log and having it bind the saw. But it's a fast way to turn trees into logs.

Getting Logs out of the Woods

As logs are cut, they should be dragged or skidded out of the woods and either stacked for air-drying or piled for loading out, as the case may be. It doesn't take

A horse — or mule — is the handiest source of motive power for skidding logs. They need no skidding roads. Photo courtesy of Boyne Falls Log Homes, Inc.

long for decay to attack a green log lying in contact with moist earth.

A horse or mule is the handiest equipment for skidding logs: they need no roads, and they can go about in any kind of weather. Unfortunately, draft animals are in short supply, and log home builders who know how to tend, harness and drive them are not exactly plentiful either. So, you will probably opt to use whatever motorized vehicle you have available that will do the job — tractor, Jeep, four-wheel-drive pickup or whatever.

Even the best of wheeled vehicles become stuck, so you'll want to schedule your skidding chores for times when the footing is relatively solid. This helps keep logs cleaner, too. (Score another point for the side in favor of cutting logs in winter, when the ground is frozen). You will also need to clear skidding trails, unless the trees in your woods are better aligned than most.

Tractors with front-end loaders, while not as maneuverable in the woods as mules, also come in handy to lift logs into position when the house goes up.

Logs should be stacked, either for air drying or temporarily while awaiting the sawmill, with no logs in contact with the ground. Notice the scrap material under the bottom row of logs in this photo, and the air space between logs in horizontal rows.

For logs that cannot be reached by vehicle, short-distance moves can be made by rolling logs with a cant hook or winching with a come-along. This is slow going, however; a power winch on a tractor or Jeep can do it faster.

Logs are easier to drag and will stay cleaner if the forward ends do not dig into the ground as they are being towed along. In rocky country, small gravels embed in the bark of logs — a situation that does not sit well with saw teeth. A log sled or boat can be built to support the end of a log being skidded, but the hood from a junked automobile will do just as well. (The tobaggon-shaped hoods of Chrysler Company cars of early-1960's vintage are particularly handy for this purpose.)

If logs are to be trucked to a mill or the building site, they should be stacked where the truck can get to them. If the truck has no hoist and no mechanical loader is available, you may want to pile logs on a road bank or build up a ramp of logs to make loading easier. Two hundred logs make quite a pile; you will probably want to load logs out as you cut them.

Where logs are to be skidded directly to the building site, they should be stacked well off the ground to allow air to circulate on all sides of each log. Lay scrap logs or poles on the ground, to support your house logs every six feet of their length. Then, stack logs in criss-cross layers, with a couple of inches of horizontal space between logs.

Ideally, logs should be seasoned for at least six months before construction begins. If you are sawing logs flat on two or three sides, they can be dried either before or after they are sawn.

After the logs have been stacked, build a framework of posts and poles over the stack and cover the logs with old galvanized metal roofing, tar paper, plastic sheeting or some other waterproof material. Build the framework tall enough so that the covering material is not in contact with the top layer of logs, so air can circulate over them, and pitch the "roof" so that water drains off.

Some authors of log-home books suggest that stacked logs be covered with grass or hay placed directly on the logs. Don't do it. Grass, hay or straw absorb and retain moisture, harbor insects and prevent air from circulating around the topmost logs.

There is no easy way to separate a log from its bark.
A sharpened tiling spade works about as well as anything
to remove large chunks of bark. Scrapers or drawknives
can smooth the job.

If you are having logs sawed or milled to a uniform thickness, save the peeling chores until afterward. The sawmill will take care of part of your de-barking problem.

The tools people use to separate logs from their bark are many and varied. A tiling spade works fairly well, followed up with a drawknife to remove stubborn patches of bark. Start the tip of the spade under the bark at one end of the log and work the bark loose in as long strips as possible. Turn the log as strips are removed.

All logs crack and check as they dry. Some species develop more and larger cracks than others, however. In general, hardwoods will crack more and take longer to season than softwoods. The cracking can be localized to some extent, by removing strips of bark on opposite sides of a log only. The logs dry faster where the bark is removed. Then, if the logs are to be sawed or hewn on two sides, many of the cracks can be carved away.

Incidentally, when you stack peeled logs for drying, it's a good idea to apply a preservative. Penta (pentachlorophenol) or copper naphthenate at a five percent solution in fuel oil can be brushed, flowed, or sprayed on (consult Appendix 1). Coal-tar creosote can also be used, diluted in equal parts of No. 2 fuel oil, but the odor of creosote is pretty strong and long-lasting. Creosote also stains logs dark.

We'll have more on preservation in Chapter 16, and simpler treatments are described in the appendix.

Peeling Logs

The bark peels easier from freshly cut logs in spring; when the sap is rising, the bark separates more readily from the cambium layer of wood. However, peeling logs — just as cutting them in the first place — is likely to be a job that is done when the builder has the time, regardless of the season.

Peeling logs is a tedious, time-consuming undertaking, whenever it is done. Some log home builders leave the bark on logs, but this is not recommended, for several reasons:

(1) as time and weather go on, the bark will begin to loosen and come off anyway — about midway through this moulting process, a log home begins to look as if it had a skin condition;

(2) leaving the bark on makes it more difficult to treat logs effectively with preservatives — wood-eating insects burrow under the bark and munch away at the sap wood;

(3) logs with bark on take longer to dry and season.

What Shape Logs?

People build homes of an almost infinite number of log shapes, styles and designs. They use round logs, square logs, half-round logs, peeled logs, unpeeled logs. They lay them up horizontally, place them vertically in a palisade-type wall — some use both styles, even in the same house.

In this book, however, we will deal primarily with buildings constructed of squared logs placed horizontally. For several reasons, logs that are squared on the facing surfaces provide a stronger, better insulated wall than round logs:

(1) their uniform thickness make a level surface for door and window frames, and make a flat, smooth plate for roof rafters or trusses;

(2) flattened logs can be fitted more snugly at wall openings and corners than round logs;

(3) flattened logs have more surface area of contact than do round logs, which makes a thicker, better insulated wall and does away with the need for a great deal of chinking between logs.

Many from-scratch log home builders use logs that have been sawed flat on two or three sides, to give a uniform thickness to logs and to provide a smooth horizontal joining surface. Logs can be sawed on all four sides for posts and beams.

Logs to be squared with broadaxe or chainsaw are accurately marked with a level, use the level to make a plumb mark on first one end of the log, then the other. Then, snap a chalk line or use a straight-edged board to mark a line the length of the log.

Except for smaller cabins completely round logs are not very satisfactory, unless tongue-and-groove or other interlocking features are milled on the facing surfaces. Some log home companies use logs of this kind, but for the builder who cuts his own logs, the interlocking features involve more work and expense than sawing or hewing logs flat on two or three sides.

So, since we are talking about a building that can be used as a full-time residence, the bulk of the construction techniques outlined refer to logs that are flattened on facing surfaces.

As we mentioned earlier, the handiest way to acquire logs that are flat on two or three sides and of relatively uniform width and thickness is to hire a saw-mill to cut your timber to specifications.

If you have the time and operating skill, you may lease or buy a sawmill — perhaps a portable mill — and saw your own logs. Another advantage of operating your own mill is the opportunity to make use of "slabs", those rounded pieces of wood that are removed from the log, for lumber, fencing, firewood or even furniture. You can also cut joists, rafters, purlins and tie beams from smaller logs. If the saw mill is in good operating condition when you are finished with your home, you should have no trouble selling it for as much or nearly as much as you paid for it.

The alternatives take more time and labor. Several milling attachments on the market let you use a chain-

Logs marked for squareness can be "scored" with a chain-saw. Carefully saw into the marks, about every 14 to 16 inches along the log. The wood between the saw cuts then is boxed out with a felling axe, and the log smoothed with a broadaxe.

saw to rip out logs or lumber, to any dimensions you wish. However, cutter teeth on standard saw chains are designed to cut across the grain of wood. If you plan to do much milling with a chainsaw, you should replace the chain with a special ripping chain.

You can hew out logs with a broadaxe, in much the same fashion that tie hackers used to make crossties for railroads. A broadaxe, as the name implies, has a wide cutting edge sharpened on one side only, to make a chisel-shaped beveled edge. The head is heavy — 10 to 13 pounds — and is set on a handle angled from the plane of the head. The offset handle prevents the hewer's knuckles from banging on the log. Broadaxes are relatively scarce these days; many of them have been bought by antique seekers. You may be able to find one in mint condition at a farm auction.

A faster way of squaring logs combines the use of both chainsaw and broadaxe. After marking the log for hewing with a chalkline or straight-edged board, "score" the log with a series of saw notches cut almost into the squaring marks. Make these notches every 12 to 16 inches along the length of the log. Then, using a regular felling axe, chop out the wood between notches until the log is roughly the dimensions wanted; finish the squaring with a broadaxe.

Whatever method you use to square logs, try to keep them to as uniform thickness as possible. This simplifies keeping the walls even as logs are laid up. An eight-foot-high wall requires 12 logs of an average eight-inch thickness. A quarter-inch difference in thickness in each log would total three inches difference in the wall.

7.

FROM-SCRATCH BUILDING BASICS

With the foundation poured, the logs cut, seasoned and squared, you are ready for the real business of building your home. Ideally, you will have thought through the stages of construction and already have decided what kind of corner notch to make, how you will tie in floor joists, what kind of subflooring you will put down, what kind of roof framing and roofing materials you will use — all these and other details should be decided before you start building. This chapter will help you finalize these plans and then put them into action.

Laying out Floor Joists

Since houses are built from the bottom up, we will start at the subflooring system — that part of the house which sits directly on the foundation.

Floor joists form a level framework over which the subfloor is laid. For general purposes, when using dimensional lumber for joists, figure on a width in inches equal to the span in feet. For example, 2X8's can be used for spans up to eight feet; 2X10's for spans of 10 feet, etc. Joists are commonly laid the short way of the area to be spanned, of course.

However, if you plan to use logs for interior partition walls, you'll want to take into account the extra weight, if those partitions are to be placed on the floor joists. It is a good idea to place partitions over a beam or girder, if possible.

Beams, either of steel or wood, are supported by concrete piers, usually poured at the same time the foundation wall is made. The beam, or girder, supports the inside end of the joists and half of the load placed on the joists. Except for log joists mortised into the girder, most construction calls for joists to overlap the top of the girder. Therefore, the girder—or beam—should be placed so as to support the inside end of joists level with the foundation wall or sill.

Many log home builders — and kit log home companies — use a standard box sill construction, then start the first course of logs on the subfloor. This method requires fewer logs, since the walls begin on top

Several methods of supporting floor joists suit log home construction. In this photo, a ledge was built into the foundation wall so that joists are flush with the top of the foundation when placed on ledge.

of the floor. The ribbon, or rim joists are usually doubled or tripled to support the added weight of log walls.

In this method of construction, a 2X6 or 2X8 is fitted over the anchor bolts and rests on top of the concrete foundation walls. Joist locations are marked off on the sill, along the longest wall.

A straight 1X3 can be marked as a layout template. With a steel square, set off the desired joist interval from one end (usually 16-inch intervals, measured from the face of a joist to the corresponding face of the next joist).

Mark the joist thickness at the end of the template as a starting point. If you are using dimensional lumber-yard joists, the thickness will be 1 ½ inches. Measure 16 inches from this, square a line across the template with a framing square and put a check mark inside the line. Repeat at 16-inch intervals.

Place the marked template against the sill, its end flush with the sill's end, and transfer the lines and check marks to the sill. The checks show on which side of the lines the joists will go — when joists are in place, they cover the check marks. In marking the opposite sill, on the other side of the house be sure to start at the same end and with the template's starting end flush with the sill. Also mark joist locations on the girder plate.

Joists should be doubled under partition walls that run parallel to them, since the load will rest on the joists alone. Either spike the joists together, or insert blocking between them to leave space for wiring or pipes, if these services must run through the wall. When doubling or tripling joists, measure the *next* joist so that all joists from the starting end fall at 16-inch intervals. To put it another way, make sure that each 16 inches along the wall marks a joist location. Disregard the doubled and tripled joists in measuring this spacing.

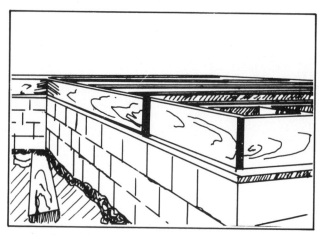

Box sill joist construction, with doubled 2x10 ribbons.

Subflooring is installed over joists; note the diagonal bridging between joists. If needed, insulation can be placed between joists before subfloor is nailed down. (Courtesy Authentic Homes Corp.)

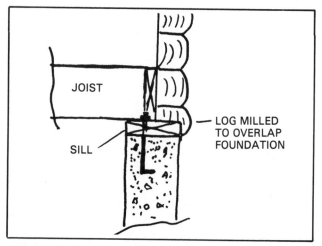

A 2x8 or 2x10 sill plate can be used, anchored to the foundation and supporting both the logs and floor joists. This method of construction is used by several log home companies. Ward Cabin Company, mills the first row of logs to over lap the sill, as shown.

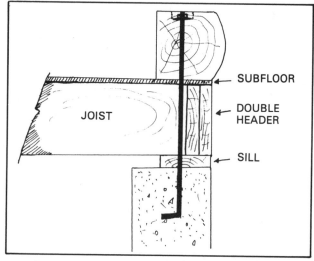

Solidly anchored, logs, subfloor and sill are bolted to the foundation wall.

Foundation types vary in log home construction. this continuous wall foundation incorporates a ledge for floor joists, which will be level with the top of the foundation. (Courtesy Authentic Homes Corp.)

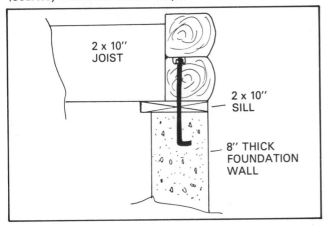

In this drawing, both the sill and first course of logs are bolted to the foundation wall.

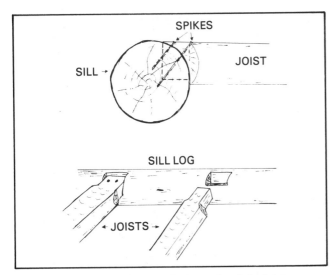

Where log floor joists are used, the ends of the joists usually are mortised into the sill log and spiked to it.

You'll also want to head off joists with double headers and trimmers around such openings as the fireplace and basement stairways. In Chapter 10, we describe how to frame out stairs. Chapter 11 discusses framing around fireplaces.

Joists should overlap the girder by about 12 inches, and should be nailed together and to the girder. To keep floor loads from twisting joists out of vertical, header joists can be spiked across the outside ends of joists. Better still, short headers of the same stock as joists (called "solid bridging") can be cut to fit snugly between each pair of joists. This takes more time, but leaves more of the sill for joists to bear on.

When the joists are in place, aligned and nailed down, you can fit bridging — the diagonal bracing between joists — down the center of each joist span. Bridging helps keep joists vertical, and to some extent transfers loads to more than one joist. You can use predrilled, custom-made metal bridging, or cut wooden bridging from 1X3 stock. The metal bridging goes in faster. Chapter 14 shows a fast, accurate way to measure and cut wooden bridging. Whichever kind you use, nail the bridging only at the top of the joist. After the subfloor is down and has some of the weight of the building on it, nail the other (bottom) end of the bridging.

Subfloor

The subflooring material — plywood or tongue-and-groove lumber, usually — is nailed on over the joists. Then, the first course of logs is either spiked or bolted to the floor framing. The most solid way to do this is to have long bolts which are embedded in the foundation wall extend high enough to anchor both the sill and the first course of logs in the wall.

Other methods of floor framing can be used. Some builders form a sort of "brick ledge" in the foundation or basement wall to support the joists level with the top of the foundation wall. Others use a wider sill, and butt the floor joists against the first row of logs. Still others use metal joist hangers to fasten joist ends directly to the bottom log, or to a header spiked to the bottom logs.

Joists made of logs are usually mortised or notched into the bottom log and spiked securely. In this method of construction, the girder usually is placed level with the bottom or sill log in the wall, and is also notched to take the inside ends of joists.

Whichever method of floor framing you choose, use joists of sufficiently heavy material and sufficient spacing to support the floor load placed on them. If in doubt about the load-carrying capacity under partitions

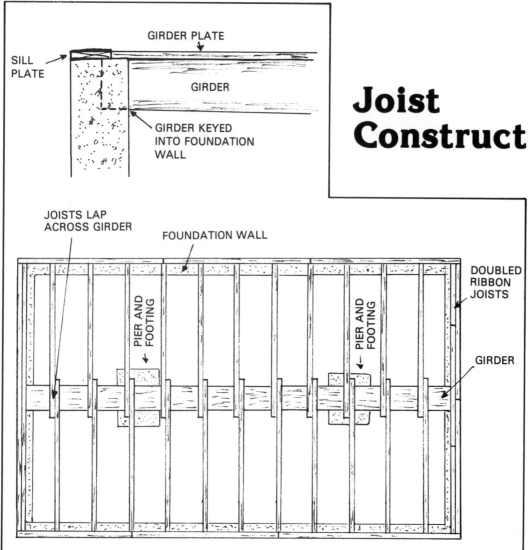

SILL PLATE

GIRDER PLATE

GIRDER

GIRDER KEYED INTO FOUNDATION WALL

JOISTS LAP ACROSS GIRDER

FOUNDATION WALL

PIER AND FOOTING

PIER AND FOOTING

DOUBLED RIBBON JOISTS

GIRDER

Joist Construction

Floor joists should lap across the girder, which is supported by the foundation wall and intermediate piers. The girder typically is keyed into a slot formed in the foundation wall so that the girder is level with the top of the foundation or basement wall.

Doubled joists which run under partitions or bear other heavy floor loads should be spiked together. Where plumbing or other utilities will run between doubled joists, separate them with solid blocks of the same material from which joist are cut.

Solid bridging, cut from the same material as joists, can be used to brace joists so they won't twist out of vertical while under loads. Depending on the construction, this solid bridging can be used to brace joists over the girder or it may be installed at the ends of joists along the foundation wall, or both.

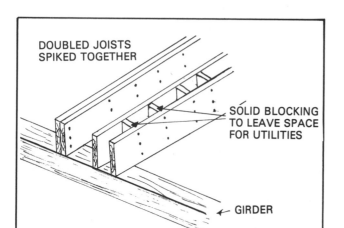

DOUBLED JOISTS SPIKED TOGETHER

SOLID BLOCKING TO LEAVE SPACE FOR UTILITIES

GIRDER

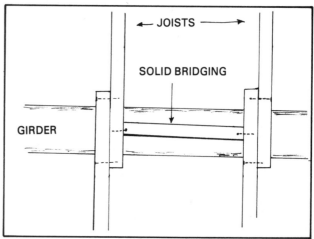

JOISTS

SOLID BRIDGING

GIRDER

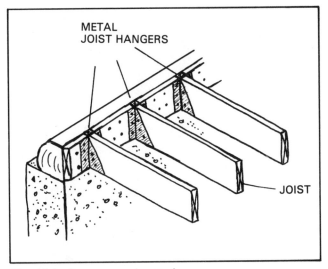

Metal joist hangers can be used.

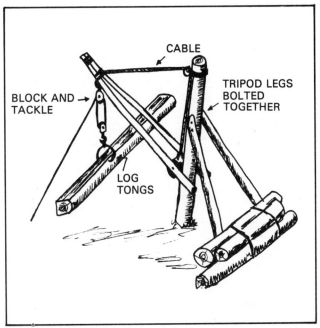

A tripod boom with block-and-tackle can be used to hoist heavy logs into position.

or areas where heavy appliances will be located, double or triple joists. Once the house is up, it's difficult and expensive to reinforce the floor framing.

Do-Ahead Work

At this point, you are ready to start up with the log walls. But let's back up first, to discuss some pre-construction procedures that will speed the actual building work. Perhaps you can take care of these while logs season, or while they are being sawed by a custom mill.

To some extent, you may be able to do part of the work on a "prefab" basis — depending on your time schedule and how well you have worked out the design of your house. You can build door and window frames and headers, to have them ready to set in place as walls go up. You can build gusseted roof trusses, or precut rafters and tie beams. You can even cut logs to length ahead of time, if your building design allows that much precision.

The more work you get done ahead of the actual building, the faster things will go at the site, of course. Chapter 14 offers additional tips about how to save time by doing some chores in advance.

Naturally, your prebuilding work will need to be done with a great deal of precision. Cutting a full set of rafters to the wrong length would waste both time and material.

Raising the Walls

Solid-log construction is not "instant" housing, even if you prefabricate some of the components ahead of time. Not when you are building a home from the ground up. It takes time to cut and fit 300- to 600-pound logs into a strong, tight wall.

It also takes power to hoist those heavy logs into position. Unless you have an army of four or five helpers, you'll need some kind of mechanical equipment — tractor with front-end loader, gin-pole type of boom and winch, an inclined ramp with block-and-tackle, etc. What you use to raise logs into walls will depend on the equipment you have available, but make sure it's heavy enough to do the job safely.

Although not the speediest method of hoisting logs, tripod swinging booms with block-and-tackle can serve the purpose. You may want to set up a boom at each wall, then move the tackle from one to the other.

Once you get the walls to the height that window frames are to be set in, you can move several logs over the low wall onto the floor deck. They will be easier to put up from the level surface inside. Be sure the floor is braced well enough to take the load.

With round logs laid up in a hurry — particularly in a smaller structure, where the logs are long enough to span one wall — it's possible to put all the logs into position, then cut door and window openings with a chainsaw. But with six- or eight-inch squared logs and

Doors and windows commonly are set in place as the walls go up, and frames serve as stiffeners to insure a plumb opening. In this Vermont Log Building, doors and windows are keyed to logs with hardboard splines. (Courtesy Vermont Log Buildings, Inc.)

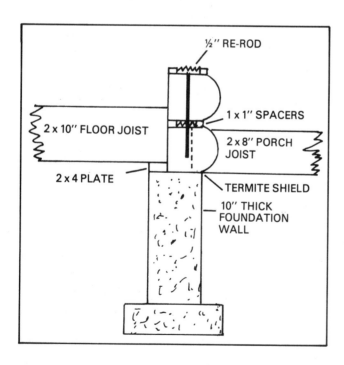

½'' RE-ROD

2 x 10'' FLOOR JOIST

1 x 1'' SPACERS

2 x 8'' PORCH JOIST

2 x 4 PLATE

TERMITE SHIELD

10'' THICK FOUNDATION WALL

This method of construction was used by Clifford Hales in building his log home. Porch joists are notched into the sill log.

walls of greater length, it's usually better to frame openings for doors, windows and fireplaces as the walls go up. In fact, the door and window frames — plumbed, leveled and well-braced — can serve as a form against which the logs are placed.

Builders who use logs sawed flat on three sides often build a form of plumbed uprights around the perimeter of the house. A chalk line is snapped along the inside wall line, and 2X4 or 2X6 uprights plumbed and braced flush with this line. Or, the first row of logs can be laid in position, and the uprights plumbed against the inside of these logs. As logs go up, they are placed into position snugly against these uprights and spiked or bolted together. It's an easy way to get a straight, plumb inside wall.

A word here about fastening logs together: some builders do not spike or pin logs together, depending on the weight of the logs to hold them in place. But it's good policy to fasten logs together every eight feet or so around the wall, and at corners and wall openings.

Bob Viebrock, who built his home of six-inch-thick logs, spiked each row of logs to the one below it with 10-inch galvanized spikes. Clifford Hales, who used squared eight-inch logs, drilled pilot holes into two or three logs at a time, then drove sections of half-inch-diameter reinforcing rod into the holes.

Tall Timber Log and Construction Company, a precut log manufacturer, uses 8-foot-long threaded rods to bolt the entire wall together at intervals of eight feet.

If you will be doing much hole-boring — pilot holes for spikes, for instance — a heavy-duty electric drill fitted with a long drilling bit comes in handy. If electrical service is not available at the site while you are building, you may want to rent one of those gasoline-engine augers utility linesmen use. The alternative is to bore holes with a hand auger or brace-and-bit.

Squared logs can be laid up one directly on the other, or can be separated with spacers made from one- or two-inch stock. Unless there is some special reason to use spacers between logs, the best bet is to place the logs in direct contact, with a gasket of urethane or other insulating material between them. The joints between logs should be caulked to make the wall water-tight.

Clifford Hales used 1X1 spacers along the inside and outside edges of logs, then filled the cavity with insulation. The reason: he wanted the appearance of masonry chinking between logs in the outer walls.

What Kind of Corner?

With round logs, the simplest and fastest corner notch to make is a round notch cut to half the diameter of the log. This notch is made only in the top log, so that the notch will face downward and not hold water. Cut the notches to fit snugly over the logs below and caulk joints well.

For squared logs, the fastest corner to make is the abutted "cob" corner, with logs in alternate courses extending a foot or so past the corner of the house. The key to making good cob corners is to measure logs carefully and cut the ends of abutting logs squarely.

An even stronger corner for squared logs can be made by notching the extended log about two inches and recessing the abutting log into this notch. Several log home companies use this type of corner. It takes more time than merely butting logs together, but the interlocking logs offer a sturdy structure.

Simple- or compound-dovetail notches make strong corners. The draw back with dovetail corners is that they have a greater horizontal-cut surface area where moisture can collect.

As much as possible, logs should be used without splices. Use the longest logs in the walls below windows; save shorter logs to fit between windows, doors and corners. A little planning can save a lot of cutting and splicing.

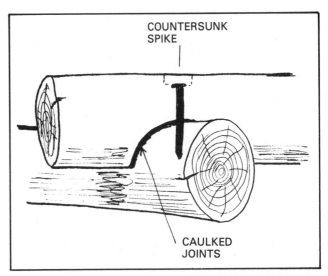

Round corner notches should be made with the notch cut into the upper log, so that moisture does not collect in the notch.

This solarized photo shows the detail of a "cob" corner notch, where intersecting logs are butted tightly together. This type of corner is popular with builders who use logs that have been sawed flat on three sides.

Doubled dovetail corner notches are somewhat complicated to fit, but when properly cut and joined they make a strong, interlocking corner. This cabin of squared pine logs is more than 100 years old.

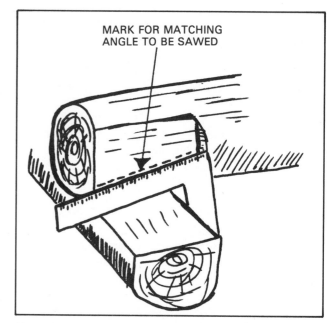

Use a framing square for marking angles in cutting dovetail notches. A steel framing square is typically 16-by-24 inches or 18-by-24 inches. The 24-inch length is the "body" and is two inches wide. The 16-or 18-inch part is the "tongue" and is 1 1/2 inches wide. The tongue meets the body in an exact right angle. Both the body and tongue are graduated in inches and fractions of an inch. Some squares also include tables such as board measurements, brace measures and rafter scales.

Fitting the Corners

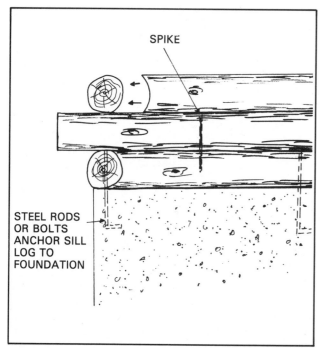

Cob corners can be made with round logs, too. The abutting log end should be cut to fit the curve of the log it joins.

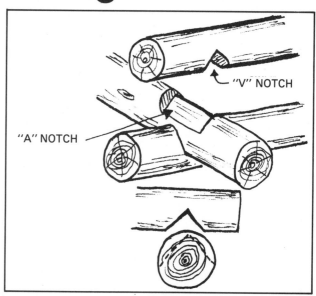

The "A" and "V" mating notches are most commonly used for round logs, but can be adapted to squared logs as well.

Wall Openings

Depending on the species of wood and how well-seasoned logs are when laid up, log walls may shrink and settle. If the settling is minor, as with seasoned softwood logs, the only result may be some fallen caulking or chinking that needs to be replaced.

However, if you expect logs to settle quite a bit as they dry in the walls, you'll need to allow space for movement over doors, windows and other openings. This can most easily be managed by fastening door and window frames to lower logs, at the bottom and on both sides, and leaving an inch or so of space between the top of the frame and the log above. Nail a drip-cap and inside trim only to this log, not to the window frame. This way, the log can move without binding the door or window. The space between the top of the frame opening and the log above should be filled with insulation.

Another solution to this potential problem is to cut a "key" way into the ends of logs that butt against the window frame. This key way will fit around a 1X1 or 1X2 spline nailed to the sides of the window frame. Then, as logs settle and shrink, they can move without binding and warping the window. This can also be done with doors and other openings.

Lay the logs up to the top of windows and doors (assuming that the tops of openings are the same height). Then on the next row of logs, the one that will form the lintel over these openings, attach metal flashing or drip-caps over doors and windows. It's easier to do this if you measure off on the log and attach the flashing to what will be the bottom side of the log when it's in place. You can use copper, galvanized or aluminum metal for the flashing.

If the roof will overhang by two feet or more, you may want to forego the flashing and merely nail a piece of 1X2 trim to the top log, to cover the space between the window frame and the log above.

Windows

Your work will be easier if all windows are of the same depth. Then if you are using logs of uniform thickness the windows all sit on the same course of logs, and are all covered by the same course of logs. This is particularly helpful if you are using window-and-frame units that can be set in place and plumbed to make a form for the logs. (For further discussion of windows see Chapter 10.)

When using these window units, make sure that windows are closed and latched, and that they are

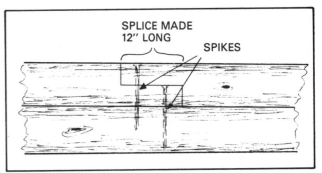

Here is one method of splicing logs in a house wall. The overlap should be cut carefully to insure a tight fit.

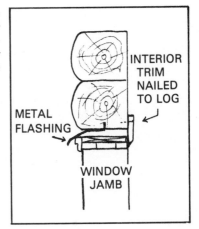

Where construction must allow for settling and shrinkage of logs, allow space above windows and doors.

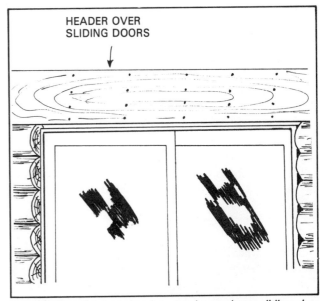

Wooden lintels, or headers, can be used over sliding glass doors to keep these opening square. These members are typically made of doubled or tripled 2x10 or 2x12 lumber, with about 3/4 inch headspace between the top of the sliding door and the lintel. Wall logs can be butted against the lintel, and the lintel can be covered with half-logs or rounded slabs for appearance.

placed rightside-up and rightside-out. (Don't laugh — it's embarrassingly easy to get one in backward or upside-down.)

Place the window unit on top of the logs it will rest on, plumb it by moving the top in or out and brace it with a length of 1X4 or 1X6 nailed to the deck. It's also a good idea to cut a stiffening spreader to nail horizontally across the window frame, about halfway up. Nail the brace to the frame at the top, not the sides. You'll need to stack logs against the side.

Sliding Glass Doors

Sliding glass doors are particularly cranky about getting out of alignment. If the frame binds even slightly out of square, they will not operate. If you are fitting wide sliding doors in your house, you may want to place a heavy metal lintel over the opening. Another way to keep the structure level and plumb is to build a header of 2X10 or 2X12 lumber, then continue the logs above this member. Obviously, above a sliding glass door is no place to splice logs.

One Story or Two?

First-floor walls should be at least seven feet, four inches high. An even eight feet can save a lot of cutting if you are planning to finish interior walls with paneling, sheetrock or other wallcovering that comes in standard eight-foot lengths.

.When the walls reach the desired ceiling height, you are ready to set second-floor joists, ceiling joists or tie beams — depending on the design of your house. If it's to be a single-story structure, you probably will frame the roof from this point, also. Or if a loft or second floor is planned, you will continue above the ceiling joists with more logs to make a full wall or stub wall, then frame the roof. Even a short sidewall, perhaps four feet high, provides more usable space in the attic than if the roof is framed from the point ceiling joists have been placed.

Where log joists are used, they are usually notched or mortised into the log wall and into a girder supported by posts in the center of the house. The girder should be 8X8 or larger. The posts supporting it normally are placed directly over the girder that runs under the first-floor joists. If a partition wall will run under the girder, it's a good idea to stud up this wall before setting the ceiling joists.

You can use a chainsaw and large chisel to make mortises at the top of the wall logs and in the girder. Make the saw notches of uniform width and depth,

Where partition walls are placed under second-floor girders, they should be erected before joists are attached to the girder.

Joists and girder should make a level surface to install subflooring or ceiling materials. In this construction, joists also tie walls together.

then chisel out the mortise. The joists should be shaped with a tenon, or tongue, that fits tightly into the mortise.

It is important that the tops of the joists and girder create a level surface on which to nail ceiling material or subflooring for upstairs rooms. Don't cut the tenons too small; use shims to level the joists.

If your design calls for the use of tie beams and purlins (horizontal roof framing members) that will be open to the ceiling, a level surface of tie beams is not at all critical.

At this point, you will also need to frame out porches and decks if these features are to be included. Then you can continue laying the walls or frame the roof, as your design requires. However, if you are

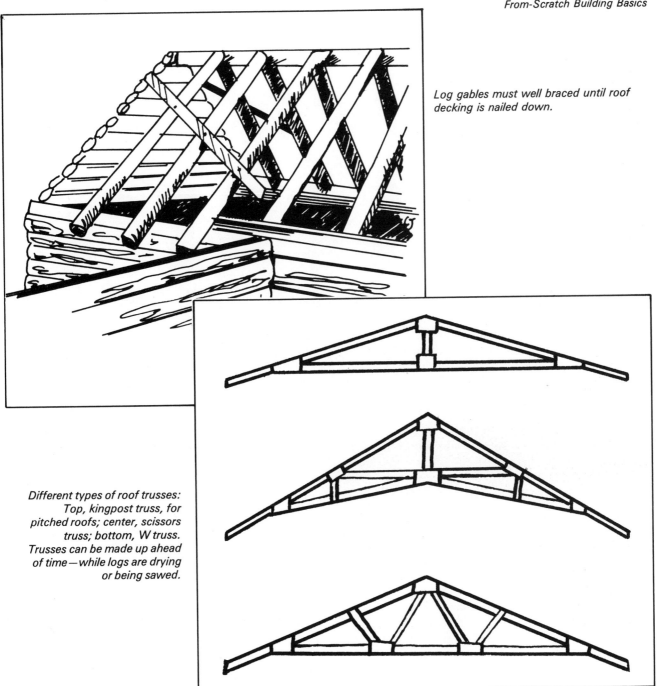

Log gables must well braced until roof decking is nailed down.

Different types of roof trusses: Top, kingpost truss, for pitched roofs; center, scissors truss; bottom, W truss. Trusses can be made up ahead of time—while logs are drying or being sawed.

building gable ends of logs, you'll want to put them in place now. It's easier to make up the gables on the level surface of plywood placed over joists, then stand the whole assembly in place. Nail a pair of rafters together to use as a pattern to assemble the gable. Plumb and brace the gables in place until the roof decking has been nailed in place.

Framing the Roof

With a one-story dwelling, you have several choices:

(1) use open tie-beams and log rafters;
(2) use gusseted trusses and conventional ceiling materials;
(3) use conventional rafters and ceiling joists; or,
(4) use a girder, log joists and log rafters, as described above.

Most log homes are built with gable roofs. These are simplest to frame and shed rain well when pitched with a wide enough angle. And a gable roof suits the overall appearance of log construction.

Of course, that does not mean that other roof styles cannot be used. Log homes are built with hip,

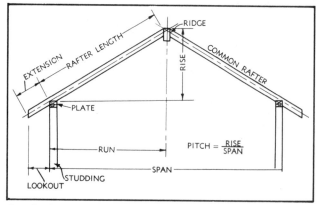

Detail of roof rise, run and overhang—or "lookout."

gambrel and mansard roofs, too. However, these roof styles require more complicated framing than do gables.

Log rafters and joists are aesthetically more suitable for a log home, but a smooth roof line is somewhat more difficult to attain than with rafters of dimensional lumber. Log rafters are also harder to cut to precise framing angles.

Whichever kind of rafters are used, they are supported by the top logs in the longer side walls. Many builders nail 2X6 plates on top of the topmost wall logs, then notch rafters to rest squarely on this plate. An alternate method that works for log rafters is to notch the top log for a snug fit by the rafters.

The slope, or pitch, of a roof is described in units of "rise" and "run". Rise is the vertical distance from the plate or top of the log wall to the peak of the roof. Run is the horizontal distance from the exterior wall to the center of the house. Pitch is expressed as a number of inches of rise for each 12 inches of run.

Suppose your house is 24 feet wide, and that the topmost point of the roof is centered and is six feet higher than top of the exterior wall. The total rise is six feet. The run is 12 feet (to the center of the building, where rafters meet). This is called a "6-in-12" pitched roof, since it rises six inches for each 12 inches of horizontal run.

The upper rafter ends meet at a ridge piece, usually constructed of a 2X8 for conventional rafters. The ridge piece should be the same length as the plate or top log.

The important angle cuts — at the ridge end of the rafter, at the notch (called a "bird's mouth") where it seats on the plate and the plumb cut at the tail — are laid out with a steel framing square. We aren't hedging the issue, but using a framing square is easier to demonstrate than to explain on paper. You may want to get an experienced carpenter to measure and cut one rafter as a pattern, then use it to cut the rest of the rafters. The measurements marked on the framing

square will aid you in determining angles, as well as lengths of rafters.

Here's a method that works for most gable-roof rafters: Make a horizontal chalk line across a wall or other smooth vertical surface. If the inside of your log walls are plumb and even, you can use an end wall. Or you can snap a line along the basement or foundation wall. Use your level to make sure the line is perfectly horizontal.

Let's assume that you are making rafters to span that 24-foot-wide house mentioned above; the one with the 6-in-12 roof. Measure off 12 feet along the horizontal line, and make marks that will represent the center of the house and the exterior wall's edge. Using a long level on the center mark, plumb a line at least six feet long. Measure six feet vertically along this line and make a mark; this mark represents the roof ridge.

Place a piece of rafter stock, or a one-inch-thick board with the same width and length as that of the rafter, at an angle so the lower edge of the board barely touches the two marks that represent the roof ridge and the wall plate. The top end of the rafter should extend past the center line by a couple of inches; the bottom end should extend past the mark that describes the plate by enough distance to provide the roof overhang you want.

With someone holding the rafter in exactly this position, transfer the center vertical mark to the rafter, by marking the top and bottom edges of the rafter where they intersect the line. Now, move to the tail of the rafter and, using the framing square against the horizontal chalk line, mark a plumb line on the rafter at the exact point that represents the outside of the wall plate. Measure off the amount of overhang you desire, then make a third plumb line to indicate the tail end of the rafter.

The rafter now is marked with three parallel lines, marking the center of the house, the edge of the wall plate and the tail of the rafter, respectively. However, at the ridge a ridgeboard will be placed between the rafters from opposite walls. The rafters will not extend quite to the center of the house at the ridge, but will need to be cut to a point that is half the thickness of the ridge piece. If you are using standard dimensional lumber, say a 2X8, for the ridge piece, mark the center plumb cut of the rafter 3/4-inch back from the original line. (Nominal two-inch lumber is actually 1½ inches thick. Half of 1½ is 3/4).

At the line which represents the exterior wall, measure and make a mark 1½ inches from the edge of the rafter so that if you are using a 2X6 plate, the 1½ inches will let the rafter notch equal the thickness of the plate. Place the framing square so that one leg lies along

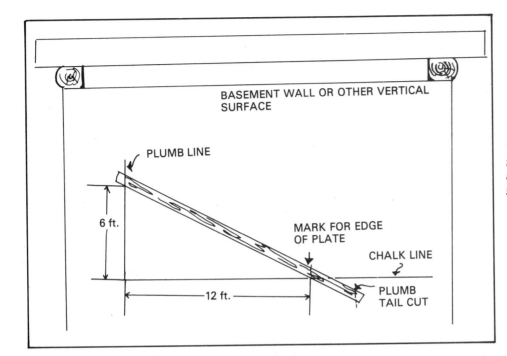

BASEMENT WALL OR OTHER VERTICAL
SURFACE

PLUMB LINE

6 ft.

MARK FOR EDGE
OF PLATE

CHALK LINE

12 ft.

PLUMB
TAIL CUT

*You can use a wall or other
flat surface to measure and
mark common rafters for
gable roofs.*

the line representing the wall and the other leg forms a right angle at the mark of 1½ inches. Draw the right angle from the mark toward the ridge end of the rafter.

The two lines you have made form a right angle — the bird's mouth — that lets the rafter sit flat on top of the plate. When the notch is sawed, the vertical cut will butt against the exterior side of the plate. The horizontal cut will lie flat on top of the plate.

The overhanging end of the rafter can be cut in, several ways, depending on how the eaves are to be finished. The accompanying sketch shows how to cut the rafter tail for a soffit — the trim member that lies between the exterior wall and the end of the rafter, on the underside of the overhang.

Cut the rafter or one-inch pattern stock according to the lines you have drawn. Make the cuts carefully through the marks; this will be the pattern by which you cut the rest of the rafters. But before you cut any more rafters, check the pattern to make sure the cuts and measurements are correct.

Measure a distance equal to the ridge height on a striaght 2X4. Plumb this 2X4 exactly in the center of the house. Sit the rafter's bird's mouth in position on the plate on top of the wall, then line up the top of the rafter's ridge end with the mark you made on the 2X4. All cuts should fit flush and even.

Some builders use log rafters which will be exposed in the ceiling, then put ceiling material over these rafters and block out above this for roof sheathing. A vapor barrier of plastic, aluminum foil or roofing felt goes on over the ceiling, and the roof is blocked out for sheathing with 2X4's or 2X6's set on edge. The space within the blocking is filled with insula-

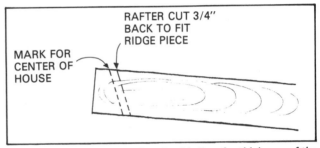

RAFTER CUT 3/4"
BACK TO FIT
RIDGE PIECE

MARK FOR
CENTER OF
HOUSE

*Plumb cut on rafter should allow for thickness of the
ridge piece.*

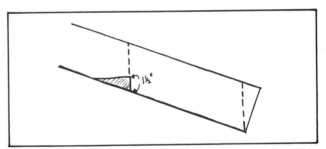

1½"

*Marking and cutting the bird's mouth to lie flat on the
wall plate.*

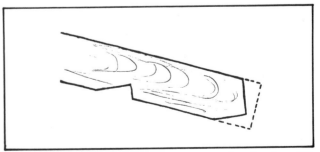

Rafter tail cut to provide a nailing surface for the soffit.

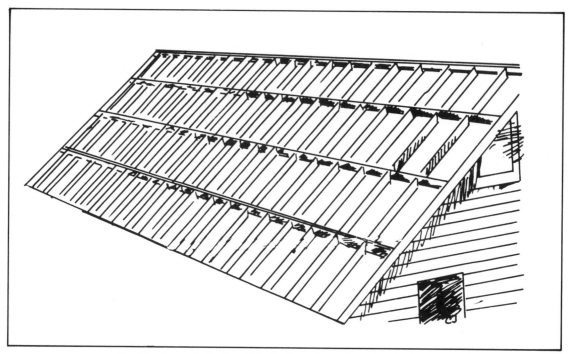

*Roof has been decked and blocked over log rafters. Insulation is placed between blocking,
then roof decking or sheathing nailed on top.*

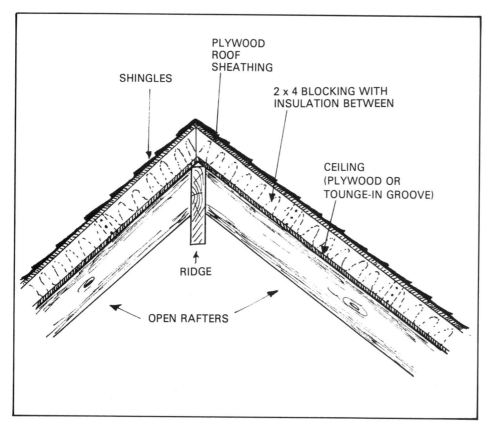

SHINGLES

PLYWOOD
ROOF
SHEATHING

2 x 4 BLOCKING WITH
INSULATION BETWEEN

CEILING
(PLYWOOD OR
TOUNGE-IN GROOVE)

RIDGE

OPEN RAFTERS

*Open-rafter ceilings can be
insulated with rigid foam or
batt-type insulating material
when the roof has been
blocked out with 2x4's or 2x6's.
Roof sheathing—usually
plywood—is nailed on over the
blocking, and shingles or other
roofing material is applied.*

tion, then the roof is decked with exterior grade plywood. Shingles or other roofing material is placed directly over the plywood. This method of roofing increases the cost of building, but combines a well-insulated roof with the rustic appearance of open log rafters.

For a single-story house that will have a finished ceiling, gusseted lightweight trusses can be used. These nailed and glued trusses are a strong, relatively inexpensive way to frame roofs, and have the added advantage that they can be made up ahead of time. Trusses incorporate both the rafters and collar or tie beams, and if properly designed, can span lengths of 30 feet with no interior bearing walls. This makes for more flexibility in planning interiors, since partitions need not be placed where they will support ceiling joists.

Gusseted trusses provide strong roof supports for log homes that will have ceilings. In the log home pictured, "W" type trusses are used.

8.

BUILDING WITH KITS

The Lincoln Log toy home kit idea has grown up into a full-fledged manufactured log home industry that has captured a good share of the single-family housing market.

Well over 100 companies are now in the precut and prefab log home business, ranging from firms with full-time designers who custom engineer homes to individual mills that specialize in cutting logs for houses. These companies are scattered from coast to coast across the U.S., as well as in many Canadian provinces.

The chief advantages of building with precut kits are savings in time and labor, plus better quality construction than might be obtained with from-scratch building projects. Two men with average construction skills, plus a couple of "fetch-it" helpers, should be able to erect the shell of a medium-sized log kit home in four days. Depending on the design and skill of the builder, it takes about one man-hour per square foot of floor area to perform the basic shell construction in a kit-built home.

Another plus for kits is their mobility: Log home builders no longer are restricted to the species of logs in their area. In many parts of the country, even heavily timbered regions, builders often prefer to use precut logs for durability or appearance.

Owners in the desert Southwest can build homes of lodgepole pine from Wyoming, or northern white cedar from Maine or Michigan. White pine and spruce logs from New England can be used to build homes in the hardwood forests of the Midwest. Richard Gerlt, whose Missouri homesite is surrounded by oak, hickory and ash trees, opted for a Boyne Falls kit home of white cedar logs.

This freedom of choice can be expensive, however. Despite the claims by some log home manufacturers, building with precut kits is not cheap. Precut homes cost from $3,000 to well over $20,000 for the kit materials, depending on the size and style of house built, and cost a dollar or more per mile to have shipped from the factory to the building site. This initial kit cost represents from one-third to one-fifth of the total completed cost, depending on how much is spent finishing out the house, its design, and how much of the work the owner can do himself.

Suppose the price for a 2,600-square-feet kit home is listed at $16,000. (That's pretty close to an average price in December, 1977.) Kits in this price range would include log walls, floor joists (for second floor only), rafters, gaskets and between-log insulation, spikes or bolts to fasten logs together, and perhaps a few other features of basic construction.

If you do virtually all of the work yourself, including much of the wiring, plumbing and interior finishing, you can expect construction to cost about 2½ times the basic kit price — or about $40,000 for the completed home. If you hire a contractor to do all the work, the completed job will cost in the neighborhood of $75,000; depending on labor costs of construction in your area. For a 2,600-square-foot house, that's right at $30 per square foot of space, and is not much different from the cost of a conventional frame house of the same square footage.

These costs do not include the cost of land, site clearing, roads or driveways, water wells and other non-building features.

The wide difference between the basic kit price and the cost of completed construction can put a builder at odds with his lender unless both parties understand that a lot of house costs a lot of money, no matter what you build with. Banks and finance companies generally make *construction* loans to finance the cost of building. Then, when the building is completed, the construction loan becomes a mortgage, which usually is paid off in equal installments over a period of years. If an owner-builder of a log kit home arranges a construction loan of $16,000 to pay for the kit we described above, then goes back later to tell his lender that he will need three to four times that amount to finish his house, the lender understandably becomes concerned about how well the builder has budgeted his costs.

So, to avoid any unpleasant surprises to yourself or your lender, figure total construction costs as accurately as possible before you order a precut log home kit.

Incidentally, import duties and provincial sales taxes increase the cost of U.S.-built kits by about 20 percent to Canadian buyers.

Ordering Kits

Start by contacting a log home company — or several — to find out if they have a standard kit model that suits your design. Most companies will make substantial changes in standard plans to suit individual requirements. Several have complete engineering and design departments, to adapt pre-cut kits to a customer's specifications.

Some companies will make preliminary scaled floor-plan drawings free of charge, with no obligation to buy a home package attached to the service. Most, however, require a signed purchase order and a minimum deposit before any plans are drawn. Ward Cabin Company will draft detailed plans, including floor plan, foundation dimensions, floor and roof framing drawings and elevation drawings for a plan deposit of $100 to $250, depending on the design. (That price is as of January 1, 1978.) This deposit then is credited to the purchase price, if a kit is bought within a year.

With costs of labor and materials steadily increasing, price lists usually carry the warning that prices are subject to change without notice. A purchase contract "locks in" the agreed-upon price, of course, even if costs go up before delivery is made.

A down payment of 25 percent when the purchase order is signed is fairly standard practice with log home companies. Most companies want the rest of their money on or before the date the first load is delivered to the building site.

Kit packages commonly are shipped on flat-bed, semi-trailer trucks, either company-owned trucks or by common carrier. In cases where shipment is most economical by rail, that form of transportation is used. Truck shipping charges are based on the actual mileage from the factory to the unloading site. The truck driver will compute the exact amount after he reaches his destination.

Where the final payment for the kit is made when the materials are delivered, Interstate Commerce Commission rules require a C.O.D. charge to be tacked onto the cost of the kit and transportation. A customer can avoid this extra charge by making the final payment a couple of weeks ahead of shipment. Then the only payment necessary when the kit is delivered will be the trucking bill. Larger homes will require two trucks — sometimes three — to haul the material.

Several log home companies, and the services and materials they feature, are listed at the end of this chapter. The list is not complete, by any means. These particular companies are chosen to give a sort of geographical representation of firms in the log home business.

Technical Help

Major log home companies or their dealers often provide a certain level of technical assistance to builders. These services range from the planning and design help in the initial stages, mentioned earlier, to on-site assistance to get the owner-builder started off smoothly. Generally, these services are included in the price for the kit package. For example, Vermont Log Buildings, Inc., provides technical help for a day or two to get construction underway.

"We provide several hours' technical assistance, when the builder requests it, whether the buyer will be doing his own building or will hire a contractor," says Jack Copeland, of Tall Timber Log and Construction Company. "We've found that buyers who build their own homes often get along better and do a better job than those who hire contractors. When a man is building his own home, he takes more time and does a more careful fitting job than some professional builders. Some contractors, unfortunately, want to get the job done in a hurry so they can move on."

Tall Timber also has construction crews that will completely close in the building shell, or do the entire construction, if the customer wants this service. These additional services, of course, are *not* included in the cost of materials.

Precut log home companies provide complete blueprints and detailed architectural plans along with their kits, and many provide materials lists and specifications for building components not supplied with the kit package.

Some companies also publish excellent step-by-step construction guides. Much of the information in this chapter is based on manuals by three of these companies: Vermont Log Buildings, Inc.; New England Log Homes, Inc.; and Authentic Homes Corporation.

Getting Ready

Site work begins with an access road to the building area. If you are putting in a new road or doing

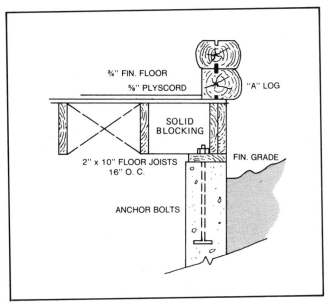

¾" FIN. FLOOR
⅝" PLYSCORD
"A" LOG
SOLID BLOCKING
2" x 10" FLOOR JOISTS 16" O. C.
FIN. GRADE
ANCHOR BOLTS

Construction details vary with kit homes. Most use a box sill method for subfloor framing, as in this sketch of a typical Vermont Log Building kit home.

extensive grading, do it early enough so that settling can take place before delivery date. The log home packages will be delivered on 40-foot flatbed trailers.

You'll also want to check the public roads to your property. They must accommodate a truck-and-trailer combined length of about 55 feet, and a weight of 60,000 pounds or so. Bridges on secondary roads often are limited to weights less than that. You may have to pick an alternate route to your building site, or get special permission from the county or state highway department to cross restricted bridges. As a last resort, you'll need to arrange for the truck to unload somewhere else, then haul the logs in smaller loads to the building site.

If the site is remote, arrange to meet the truck at a convenient point and pilot the driver in.

You will also need enough cleared area at the site for trucks to maneuver into position and unload. Remove and trim up trees. Protect any trees you want to save with temporary fencing, or band them with 2X4's.

The foundation — slab, crawl space or full basement — is your responsibility, too. With few exceptions, log home companies and their dealers do no concrete work. You will receive a set of foundation drawings from the company well ahead of time. These blueprints will specify any special features that need to be incorporated into the foundation. Some kit plans require a "brick ledge" sort of off-set in the foundation,

on which to place floor joists. Have the foundation poured and forms stripped from the concrete before delivery date. You may also want to back-fill around the foundation, to make a more level surface on which to work.

With many precut kits the subflooring system — beams, joists and floor decking — should be constructed before the package arrives. The blueprints provided by the company will indicate the type of floor framing to use. Most specify the box sill method described in Chapter 7.

Tools to Have on Hand

The tools you need to erect a log home kit are, in general, those you would use for any other house construction. It is a good idea to gather the following tools and have them on hand when the truck arrives, so construction work can begin right after unloading:

- 6 or 8 lb. sledge hammers — two of them, for driving spikes;
- 3-foot pinch bar — for moving logs and for removing spikes that have been driven in the wrong spots;
- 3-foot level — to check plumb of doors and windows;
- staple gun or staple hammer — for tacking gasket material;
- ratchet winch and 30 feet of rope — for pulling logs tightly together;
- 50- or 100-foot steel tape — for checking various building dimensions;
- a carpenter's claw hammer — for nailing decking, window frames, etc;
- handsaw or power saw — for cutting joists, plywood, etc;
- framing square — for checking square on doors and windows;
- wide-bladed wood chisel — for cleaning mortise cuts;
- drawknife — for trimming logs and removing bark;
- chalk line — for "snapping" lines to align building members.

Other equipment and material that may come in handy includes:

- small chainsaw for cuttings larger fireplace opening
- caulking gun

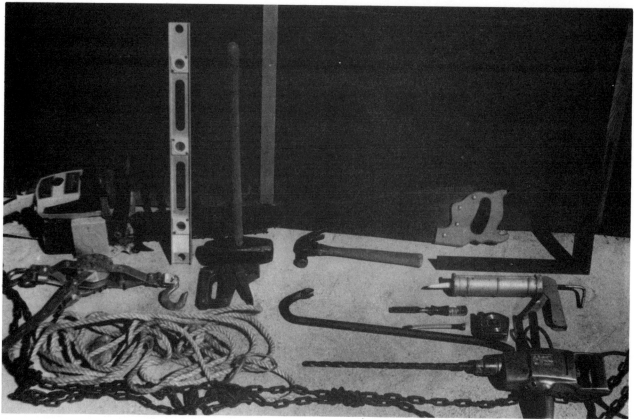

Some of the tools needed to erect a precut log home.

- wire cutters
- electric drill and bits
- flashing for termite shield
- tin snips to cut the flashing
- supply of 2x4's and 1x4's for bracing and framing
- nails (a good supply of 16d and 8d commons, plus a few 20d and 40d)
- conduit (if needed for electric runs)
- hacksaw to cut the conduit
- dunnage or scrap lumber (such as 4X4's) to support the logs off the ground

Unless the log home company's truck has an unloading hoist, you will need to arrange for equipment or manpower to unload the truck. The driver is not responsible for unloading, and except for untying the load, most probably will not volunteer to help.

Kit logs normally are banded together in bundles of 16 to 20 pieces each. The bundles weigh from 1,500 to 3,500 pounds. It speeds unloading if you have the use of a forklift or crane for this ceremony. However, such components as windows and doors should be unloaded by hand, to prevent damage.

D Day

On delivery day, have the equipment and helpers assembled before the truck arrives; you will be notified of the delivery date and time well in advance. Company trucks, barring road trouble, usually hit their expected arrival time pretty well on the dot. Common carriers are not always so punctual.

Long-range weather cycles are ignorant of delivery dates. Neither you nor the log home company nor the truck driver can do much about the weather. But you can have a contingency plan ready — just in case roads are icy or muddy.

Unless you have made final payment for the kit in advance, you'll need a certified check for the balance due, plus the freight charge, if the load is delivered by company truck. If a separate freight company does the hauling, you will need two checks — one for the company and one for the trucker.

When the truck arrives, check the condition of the material before the driver unstraps the logs and other packages. If the load has been wedged in an underpass enroute, now is the time to make a note of any damaged material. See that the driver acknowledges the damage, too. Whether or not you accept damaged material is up to you. You may unload the material, then file a freight damage claim. Or, you can refuse delivery. In either case, notify the company or its representative as soon as possible.

Unload the truck as quickly as safety will allow. With a forklift or tractor and front-loader to handle the logs, a 40-foot trailer can be unloaded in about two hours. Stack the logs on scrap lumber or dunnage to keep them out of the dirt.

A materials check-off list will accompany the load. It is a good idea to have one person check off items as they are unloaded.

Getting Started

Sorting the Logs

Once the trailer has been unloaded, the driver paid and on his way, it is time to start sorting the logs. Most companies number or letter each log to indicate its location in the wall. However, the logs will have been grouped into bundles for easy shipment. You must pick through the bundles to sort and stack all "A" logs together, all "B" logs together, and so on.

Refer often to your blueprints or construction guide. Each course of logs will have the same letter or number. Sort them so that the logs for the bottom courses are handiest to the building. If your subflooring is already down, you can stack the first three or four courses right on the deck. (If you place many logs on the decking, you may want to add some temporary bracing under the floor before hand).

Joists should be sorted by length, and rafters should be separated by type and length. Porch and deck materials, if included in the kit, should be separated from joists and rafters. Windows and doors should be stored upright and off the ground.

Laying Logs

The blueprints and construction guides will indicate whether sill members are to be placed under the first course of logs. Where a box-sill subfloor is used, logs normally are started directly on the decking.

Lay out all of the first course of logs before spiking or drilling any of them. Make sure that you have laid the logs in the proper sequence, from the right starting point, and that all logs are for the first course. Doors, or door frames, usually are set in place on the sill or subfloor before logs are placed. Check the inside

Kit logs are engineered for a tight fit, and most are joined splines, tongue-and-grooves or other interlocking surfaces. (Courtesy Vermont Log Buildings)

Each log in a home kit is coded to identify its position in the building. (Courtesy Authentic Homes Corp.)

Many kit homes specify that gaskets or insulation material be attached to logs as they are placed. (Courtesy Authentic Homes Corp.)

dimensions of the width and length of the building. If everything is right, then start spiking or bolting the logs

A few log home companies use round logs, joined on facing surfaces with tongue-and-grooves or splines. Pictured is typical Beaver Log Home construction.

to the sill or foundation wall, as the kit instructions indicate.

Many kits require that pilot holes be bored for spikes or bolts. High-speed twist drill bits work better for this than ''spade'' type boring bits. Your blueprints will show what size spikes to use and the distance apart they are to be spaced.

After the first course of logs has been laid, checked for dimensions and anchored down, continue laying up logs in the sequence indicated on the blueprints. Check the width and length dimensions as each course of logs goes up. A ''come-along'' or ratchet winch and a length of rope can be used to snug logs into position.

Tie the rope around the log ends at each corner of the wall, attach the rachet winch and pull logs together to seat them firmly against door and window openings; however, do not apply so much pressure that door and window frames buckle or warp. This technique is used by log home companies, and is particularly helpful when compressible gasket material is used between logs and framed openings.

When you come to the window courses of logs (that row of logs on which window frames will be placed) make sure the windows are plumbed and aligned properly. Most kits use splines, tenons or other features to secure jambs to log walls. These are designed for a tight fit.

Except for the special features engineered into different log kits, the same construction principles apply

Wilderness Log Home utilizes round logs, with insulation and caulking between logs. (Courtesy Wilderness Log Homes)

Ward Cabin Company uses squared, white cedar logs with interlocking corners.

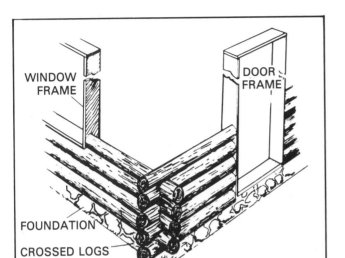

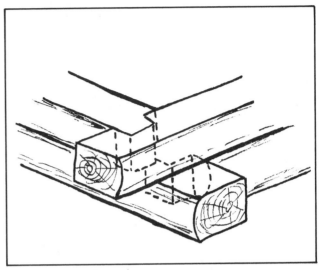

Any builder with moderate construction skill can build his own kit log home. Blueprints and technical instructions provide step-by-step guides. (Courtesy Vermont Log Buildings)

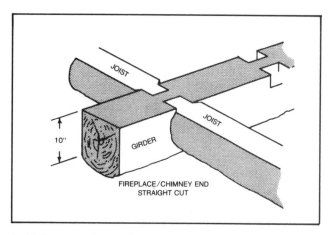

In kit home packages, logs, girders, joists and rafters are precut for a precise fit. (Courtesy Vermont Log Buildings)

as for from-scratch log homes. All components are designed and cut to fit together. If you put everything in its right place at the right time, the construction of your kit log home should go smoothly.

But everyone makes mistakes, and you may find a piece that has been cut too short, too narrow or to the wrong angle. Refer to the blueprints and double-check your own measurements and construction to this point. Then, if it's still out of whack, contact the company or their representative.

The precut log homes manufactured by major companies are strong, solid, permanent structures. The best of them will be standing and serviceable long after many of their frame-built counterparts have collapsed.

Authentic Homes Corporation's ''Seneca'' model ranch style home, under construction and completed. Kit price for the 1,793-square-foot Seneca shell is $12,690 (as of February, 1978). The two-car garage kit goes for $3,960. (Courtesy Authentic Homes Corp.)

Selected Manufacturers of Precut Log-and-Kit Homes

New England

New England Log Homes, Inc.
P.O. Box 50562
Hamden, Connecticut 06518
    Hand-peeled pine logs, squared on two sides and joined with splines; kits; custom design services.

Northeastern Log Homes, Inc.
Groton, Vermont 05046
(Also at Kenduskeag, Maine; and Louisville, Kentucky)
    Milled Eastern white pine logs, joined with tongue-and-grooves. Kits; custom planning services.

Vermont Log Buildings, Inc.
Hartland, Vermont 05049
    Machine-peeled pine logs; joined with splines. Kits; full custom planning services.

Ward Cabin Company
Box 72
Houlton, Maine 04730
    Hand-peeled northern white cedar logs, joined with double tongue-and-grooves and interlocking corners. Kits; custom design services.

South:

Arkansas Log Homes, Inc.
Mena, Arkansas 71953
    Machine-peeled, squared pine logs joined with splines. Kits; custom design services.

Beaver Log Homes, Inc.
P.O. Box 1145
Claremore, Oklahoma 74017
    Machined, round pine logs with double tongue-and-groove joints. Kits; custom design services.

Carolina Log Buildings, Inc.
Box 368
Fletcher, N.C. 28732
    Machine-peeled, squared pine logs. Kits; design services.

Eureka Log Homes, Inc.
Berryville, Arkansas 72616
    Pine or hardwood peeled logs; kits; design services.

Frontier Log Cabin Homes
Box 96
Ingram, Texas 78025

Heritage Log Homes
P.O. Box 610
Gatlinburg, Tennessee 37738
    Double tongue-and-grooved pine logs. Kits, plans services.

Tall Timber Log and Construction Co.
Route 3
Boonville, Missouri 65233
    Milled tongue-and-groove cedar logs; construction services.

West:

Air-Lock Log Company
P.O. Box 2506
Las Vegas, New Mexico 87701

Alpine Log Homes
P.O. Box 85
Victor, Montana 59875

Authentic Homes Corporation
P.O. Box 1288
Laramie, Wyoming 82070
    Flattened, peeled logs cut from standing dead ponderosa and lodgepole pine. Kits; custom design services.

National Log Construction Company
Box 68
Thompson Falls, Montana 59873

Pan Adobe
4350 Lake Washington Blvd., N.
Renton, Washington 98055
    Squared, tongue-and-grooved Western red cedar logs. Planning services.

Real Log Homes, Inc.
Missoula, Montana 59807
    Machine-peeled, squared pine logs. Kits; design services.

Central:

Boyne Falls Log Homes, Inc.
U.S. 131
Boyne Falls, Michigan 49713
Hand-peeled northern white cedar logs joined with double tongue-and-grooves. Kits; custom design services.

Wilderness Log Homes
Route 2
Plymouth, Wisconsin 53073
Round peeled pine and cedar logs; also a "half-log" model with framed walls. Kits; planning services.

This two-story log home nestles into the Ozark mountain woods.

Shown are double-dovetail corners on square pine log cabin; logs are stained redwood.

Rain gutters that carry water away from house and foundation, prevent wood decay and thus add to the life of a log home.

Log ceiling joists in place.(Courtesy Vermont Log Buildings, Inc.)

A double-deck home combines beauty with utility; note through-wall room air-conditioners. ▶

Dark-stained logs on this Beaver Log Home set off dark mortar in fireplace.

Home over a walk-out basement is offered by Beaver Log Homes.

9.

RECYCLING AN OLDER LOG BUILDING

Restoring older homes—log and otherwise—to full time use is gaining popularity all over the country. It's a trend that can give a handy man (or woman) a definite edge aginst inflation, since housing investment returns outpace most other other price increases. And for the log home owner it can provide a live-in history not available from a new home.

Almost any remodeling project presents unique problems; each undertaking is the only one of its kind. This is doubly true of older log houses. The work involved to rehabilitate and modernize a log home can range all the way from scraping and rechinking the logs, and perhaps modernizing the plumbing and wiring, to completely dismantling and cataloging the parts of an old cabin or other building and then incorporating the useable pieces into a new structure.

Because each rebuilding or remodeling enterprise is different from every other, we outline in some detail what you are likely to encounter in an older log building, as well as some suggestions on how to handle the more general problems that arise.

Later in this chapter we also report the experiences of two builders who have rebuilt log homes that were originally constructed more than 100 years ago. You will experience no exact replay of what these two builders encountered, nor will you end up with an exact duplicate of the homes that resulted from their efforts. But the fact that these families successfully rebuilt homes—each more than a century old—is proof that it can be done.

Finding Older Log Buildings

Your chances of finding a rebuildable older log structure depend partly on where you choose to live. There are few existing log cabins on the High Plains, for instance; settlers in these tree-scarce regions constructed their homes of sod. The same is pretty much true of the arid Southwest, where adobe structures sheltered early settlers.

Even in the more timbered sections of North America, log buildings are not always plentiful. You will need to search some to find a log structure that is worth the time and effort of rebuilding. You may have to search even harder to find a for-sale log home on an acreage of land that also is available.

Start your search among local realtors and newspaper classified ads. Occasionally, private owners will advertise a house or other building that must be moved. At times, farms and family estates will be sold in pieces. You may find a 10- or 20-acre tract with an older log building that can be bought separately from a larger parcel of land. The odds aren't great—in most regions—that many houses you will find this way will be log structures, but it is a place to start. A quick visit to local realtors can determine if any properties with log homes are listed.

While looking through area newspapers, check for stories about businesses or public works that plan expansions or new construction. Existing homes must make way for freeways, highways, lakes, airports, shopping centers, hospitals, schools and other developments. In most cases, it is cheaper for the planners of the new construction to let you move a condemned building than it is for the company to tear the structure down. These buildings often can be bought for the cost of the paperwork necessary to transfer ownership—perhaps $50 or less.

Next, check among the supervisors and managers of public lands in your region—national park superintendents, state park managers, national forest rangers, etc. Often, long-term leases are granted to home builders on public lands. These leases expire or often carry a provision that the original lessee cannot transfer the lease. In these cases, the cabin or other structure that was built on public lands becomes public property, and may be for sale on a sealed bid basis. Public areas where the use of the land is being changed are good places to look for buildings; for example, where public forest lands are being converted to a wildlife refuge or recreational area.

You need not limit the hunt to buildings originally constructed as dwellings. All sorts of second-hand materials can be useful: Old bridge timbers, barn beams, utility poles and railroad crossties are reincarnated as log walls, girders, beams and joists in log homes.

One Illinois builder salvaged black walnut posts and beams from his grandfather's barn for use as open girders, beams and a fireplace mantel in his new log home. Not only would it have been terrifically expensive to buy walnut for these members today, but the Illinoisan has incorporated family history into his home as well.

Another imaginative log-home seeker, a New Mexico stockman, built an 80-foot-diameter round horse barn—complete with show arena—from railroad ties salvaged from a spur track that had been abandoned. The ties were cut in half lengthwise, then laid up in mortar—concrete block fashion—to make a unique, weathertight shelter for the Southwesterner's show horses.

As you search out and inspect older buildings for

potential recycling, don't concentrate on the logs alone. Old doors, windows, framing and other features from existing buildings are often re-used in brand-new homes. Conversely, in a rebuilding project, deteriorated or badly warped doors can be replaced with new doors made from tongue-and-groove lumber or old barn siding with the edges planed for a tight fit. These new doors, door and window frames and other brand-new

Probe logs at corners, window and door openings and around the foundation for rotted wood. These areas are particularly vulnerable to decay and weather damage.

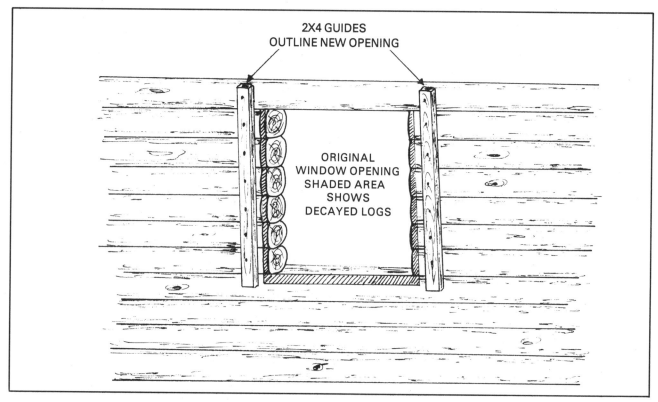

Logs adjacent to window and door openings may rot at the ends, while the rest of the log is still sound. In these cases, opening for new windows and doors can be cut enough larger to reach solid wood.

construction added during the rebuilding of an older house can be "weathered" and stained to suit the appearance of the original wood in the building. We'll go into this more fully later.

Inspecting Your Find

Whether you now own an older building or locate one which can be bought, inspect the structure closely before you decide to try to remodel or rebuild it. Some buildings can be rejected immediately; they would not be worth the effort to rebuild even if the building could be obtained without cost. And, if you find a building that stands in the way of "progress" and must be moved, you may find that only a relatively small part of the building is worth the time and cost of tearing it down and hauling it away. In any case, you will want to examine the structure carefully before you agree to buy it—or even take it as a gift. Examine these features thoroughly before you decide. The top and bottom of a building can reveal much about its structural soundness. You can see more of the construction details in the attic, on the roof and in the basement or crawl space than anywhere else.

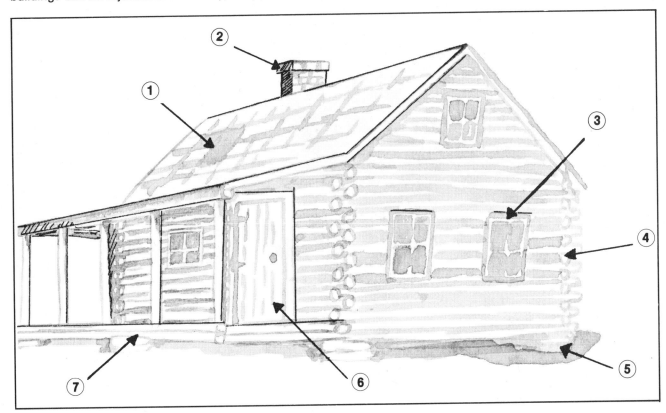

Inspection of an existing log building should focus keen attention on these areas:

(1) *loose shingles or other damaged roofing; evidence of leaking;*

(2) *chimney cap, look for loose mortar, clogged flues, check the flashing between chimney and roof;*

(3) *windows and frames, inspect for signs of decay, warping indicates log walls are settling;*

(4) *corners provide a lot of surface area for weather to attack, look for rotted, decayed wood;*

(5) *foundations and basements or crawl spaces require close examination, look for rotted sills and beams, evidence of termites;*

(6) *exterior doors may be sagging, check to see if doors have been planed recently; and*

(7) *porches and decks should be examined, top and bottom, for decaying wood, particularly in floor framing members.*

Roofs are another likely trouble spot with older buildings. Here, the roof covering has been removed to expose sheathing boards and rafter ends. Note the sagging roof line at the ridge.

Roof and Attic

On the roof and in the attic, look for evidence of long-term leaks. If the shingles or other roof covering have been in bad shape for some time, you may need to replace everything from the tops of the walls up—ceiling joists, ceiling material, rafters, roof sheathing, roofing. While you are up there, check the condition of the chimney and flues. Is the mortar loose and crumbling? Is the flue open? Is the flashing between the chimney and the roof in good shape?

Foundation and Flooring

Under the house, look first at what kind of underpinnings the building has. Is it on a foundation or solid masonry piers, or merely propped up on a few flat stones? How about the sill logs and beams under the center of the house? Probe the wood of these members with a knife or screwdriver. Look for evidence of rot or termite damage, as described in Chapter 3. You can get a good look at the subfloor, too; which may tell you more than the carpeting, linoleum or tile that covers it.

Around the outside of the house, inspect the condition of the logs and chinking. Look closely at the corners, where more wood is exposed to weather. Check the condition of exterior door and window frames. Inspect the porch and its supporting members.

Inside the house, check to see that flooring is sound and reasonably level. Doors and windows should fit snugly and operate freely. If not, it may mean that walls have settled and skewed out of alignment. Check areas around sinks, bathtubs and other places where water may leak. Suspect any areas where the wood is discolored, or where the floor feels spongy under your step.

Utilities

How about utilities? The house may need to be rewired (in all probability, it will require this) and possibly equipped with heavier-duty electrical service for modern appliances. Is the plumbing in good shape? Can the water lines be protected from freezing? What kind of sewer system does the building have? What kind of heating system? Inspect the furnace, if one is installed, and the ductwork.

The log sills and joists, as well as the decking on this old porch are too far gone for anything but firewood.

If you will need more space than the house provides, consider whether the design and condition of the building lend themselves to additions. Is there enough space to build a deck, porch or patio to extend the fair-weather living space?

Decision: Remodeling without Moving the House?

Of course, the emphasis you put on different features of the house during your inspection depends on whether you will remodel the house in place or move it to another location. After you have inspected and re-inspected the building from top to bottom and back again, you may decide that the house can be remodeled without tearing it completely down and rebuilding.

However, it is doubtful that you will want to leave the space exactly as it is. You may want to knock out a wall to enlarge the kitchen, or put in a wall to subdivide a larger space. You may want to build dormers in the roof to create additional usable space in the attic. Or you may decide to add a room or section of framed or log construction to expand the living space.

Scale Drawing

It is important that you start any remodeling job with a scale drawing of the house as it is now, in order to plan any changes you will make. This is helpful procedure even if you plan to remodel only a part of the house. By studying the entire floor plan, you can better fit the remodeled area into the overall plan of the house.

A scale drawing of the present layout is simple: Use plain paper, or use a special cross-sectioned paper divided into eight squares per inch. You will also need a straightedge, pencil, eraser (we all make mistakes) and a 25- or 50-foot measuring tape. Use a steel tape; fabric tapes can stretch enough to give incorrect measurements, and you will want to be as exact as possible.

Make your drawing to some scale that is easy to interpret. A scale of one-fourth inch equal to one foot is handy. It's helpful if one person does the drawing and two get the dimensions. On your drawing, show partitions as near their thickness as possible; most are about six inches thick. It is also a good idea to show the direction of floor joists on the plan, and to indicate load-bearing walls. This information is helpful later, if you decide to knock out a wall or add a new one.*

*All exterior walls are load-bearing walls. Any interior wall that runs at right angles to the ceiling joists will be a load-bearing wall, holding up the joists.

When all the information has been placed on the "before" drawing, you can start drafting a working plan of what the house will look like "after." Unless you are doing a thorough-going remodeling job, you will probably want to "design around" such features as stairways, fireplaces, doors and windows, rather than try to relocate them. Use tracing paper to duplicate the present drawing, then make sketches of remodeling details. The original plan should be preserved as is, as a reference.

When the overall plan has been developed, you may want to make detailed drawings of individual rooms to larger scale. Kitchens, bathrooms and other rooms with a lot of planning detail may require overlays of tracing paper, to show plumbing runs, electrical wiring, and other features.

Decision: Move a House—Intact or in Pieces?

Log houses are not the most mobile of structures, certainly not if the entire building is to be moved at once. It can be done, but be prepared for a shock if you hire professional movers to relocate a house of any size. The tab can run to $1,000 *per mile* or more.

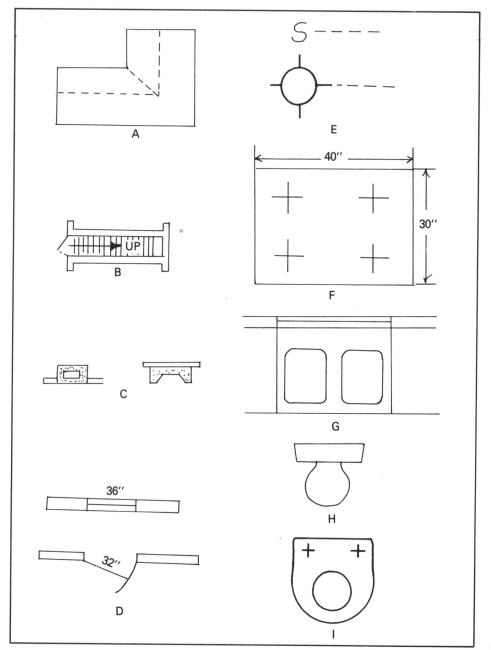

Here are handy symbols for indicating features of a home scheduled for remodeling: (A) the roof line of the house should be shown, showing amount of overhang and ridge lines (B) stairways are measured and drawn, with an arrow to show stair direction; (C) Indicate the location and size of fireplaces and chimneys, (D) windows and doors can be shown this way, (E) electrical switches, outlets and light fixtures and the location of wiring runs should be shown, use "S" for switches, an "O" for light fixtures and a square for all outlets; (F) kitchen appliances should be drawn in to scale, as should (G) sinks and cabinets; (H) and (I) mark the location of toilets and lavatories, respectively.

It is cheaper, and usually more satisfactory, to disassemble a log building, then reassemble it at the new site. This does not mean that it is easy to move an old log cabin—even in pieces.

If the building is to be reassembled pretty much as it now stands, it is important that each piece be marked as it is taken down. Older, handmade log homes were not built with the uniform logs and precision corner notches of modern kit-built homes. Therefore, each log must be put back in precisely the same place and in the same position if it is to fit properly. Later on in this chapter, we tell how a Houston architect, Carroll Tharp, goes about moving and rebuilding log houses. You will pick up several valuable tips from Tharp's experience.

Reconditioning

Reconditioning an older log house is a different proposition from redoing a frame home where the walls present a plane, flat surface that can be doctored with paint or paneling. Refer to Chapters 7 and 8 for basic construction details on those features that need complete rebuilding from scratch. For example, if the roof and rafters need to be replaced, it's simpler to remove everything to the top or plate log and rebuild with new rafters, gusseted trusses or other new members.

The problems you will encounter will depend on the general condition of the log house you set out to rebuild, of course. But here are some of the more common defects found in even those log buildings that are fairly sound structurally:

Walls

The most common malady in older log homes is loose chinking between the logs. Many older cabins were built with unseasoned logs and wide spaces were left between the logs to allow for settling and shrinkage. Originally, these cracks probably were chinked with a mixture of straw and mud (or clay), and your cabin may still have this kind of chinking—or vestiges of it.

Mud chinking, of course, should be completely removed. Even where the mud chinking later has been replaced with mortar, the chinking may be cracked and loose. The best bet is to remove all of it and replace it. You will need to remove the chinking anyway, if you plan to clean the logs.

Scraping Bark. If the house is built of peeled logs, the wood will probably have darkened with age. If you want a fresh, new appearance to logs—inside, outside,

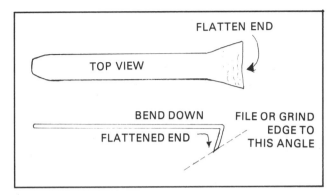

Log scrapers can be made from sections of car springs or old files, heated and flattened on one end. Bend the flattened end to slightly more than a right angle and sharpen a beveled edge.

or both—a metal floor scraper or cabinet scraper and a lot of elbow grease can restore them. Or, if the weathered look is preferred, scrape only enough to remove all old chinking and to make a solid surface on log edges to hold the new chinking.

If the logs originally were laid up with the bark on, you may encounter more trouble. For one thing, wood borers and other insects will probably have infested the sapwood directly beneath the bark. These pests chew holes and trenches in the wood. The bark should be removed completely, and the logs scraped to remove all of the sapwood that has been damaged by insects.

A good scraper can be made from an old flat file, or from a section of leaf spring from an old car chassis. Heat the metal and flatten one end to a thin edge, then bend about one inch of the flattened end down as shown in the accompanying drawing. Sharpen the scraper edge on one side only, then draw the tool along the length of a log to carve away the bark and about a quarter-inch of the sapwood beneath.

After the bark and damaged sapwood have been scraped away, use a cabinet scraper or small floor scraper to smooth out any gouged and grooved places in the logs. Then, use a steel wire brush to remove the dust and chips. If you wish, you can go over the entire surface of the logs with an electric wire brush to brighten them, then finish or preserve the logs as mentioned in Chapter 16.

Rechinking. When the logs have been cleaned, you're ready to fill the gaps between with new chinking. The material used to chink spaces between logs should seal out both air and water. Caulking compound can be used to seal narrow cracks, but for wider spaces a rich cement mortar is the most popular choice. However, before the mortar is applied, some sort of "lath" should be installed to hold the mortar in place. Metal hardware

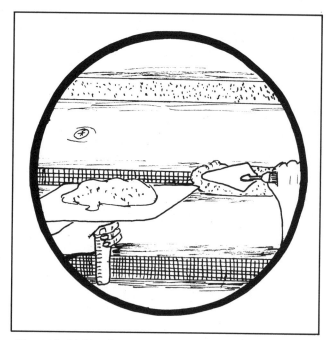

After old chinking is removed and logs are cleaned, you may want to nail some kind of "lath" to hold the new mortar used in rechinking. Metal hardware cloth works well.

cloth, cut into long strips and stapled or tacked in place, works very well.

If you plan to chink both the inside and outside of the walls, you will probably want to chink exterior walls first and then apply chinking to the interior. If the logs are large enough, you may place fiberglas or other insulation in the gaps after the outside chinking is installed. As an alternative to chinking the interior walls, the gaps between logs can be covered with thin batten boards, or other trim, stained to match the logs.

For mortar chinking, mix equal parts of Portland cement and clean, sharp sand. The easiest way to apply the mortar is with a small pointed trowel. A plasterer's hawk is handy for holding a supply of mortar while you're working, and for catching the mortar that falls off the trowel. Start at the top of the wall and work down. If finished floors have been installed, you will want to protect them when chinking the interior walls.

Floors

Unless floors have been replaced since the house was originally built, most older homes will have wooden floors—many of them covered with worn, scaling linoleum. If the old floors are not too badly worn, warped or rotted, you may be able to sand them with a power floor sander and finish the floor boards. In most areas, you can rent sanding machines.

Sand the wood carefully to provide a smooth surface. Any irregularities will be magnified by the finish. The last sanding should be with 2/0 grit sandpaper, and all dust should be vaccuumed up or cleaned up with an oiled rag.

If a highly polished surface is to be applied, hardwood floors will need a filler coat to close pores in the wood. Brush a liquid filler on liberally, first across the grain of the wood, then with the grain. When the glossy wet sheen is gone, wipe up the excess filler. Allow the filler to dry completely before applying stains or varnishes.

If the flooring boards vary in color and shade, you may want to use a stain to get a more uniform color. If the natural color of the wood is desired, finish the floor with varnish or sealer (a thinned coat of varnish). Apply the finish evenly, let it dry thoroughly, and apply a coating of wax.

If the existing floor is sound but not suitable for refinishing, you can lay new flooring — either hardwood or softwood — crosswise over the old boards. Or, if vinyl, linoleum or carpeting will be used, you may first want to cover the old floor with particleboard, underlayment. Don't put floor coverings over rough, badly warped flooring; such a surface makes carpeting and linoleum short-lived.

Ceilings

For open-beam ceilings that need work, a quick answer is to nail 4x8 sheets of Celotex or other insulating board right over the old ceiling. (Note: Use short nails if there is danger of the nails penetrating the roof.) The joints and nailing areas of the ceiling material can be covered with batten boards for a beamed effect.

If you want more "wood" look overhead, you can install tongue-and-groove boards over the old ceiling. For the existing ceiling in an open-rafter or open beam house that has no insulation, you may want to fur with 2x2 strips, install rigid insulation, and then nail the tongue-and-groove ceiling boards in place.

For older houses with conventional ceilings that need to be replaced, you can go one of several ways. If the ceiling is high — i.e., eight feet or more from the floor — you may want to install a suspended ceiling, perhaps with recessed lighting panels. It is also a simple matter to staple batt-type insulation behind the gridwork that supports the ceiling panels (keeping the vapor barrier facing down into the room). Or, you can install one-foot-square insulating ceiling tiles directly over the old ceiling.

You may be lucky enough to get by with merely cleaning and painting the ceiling. Use your imagination in choosing bright or pastel colors that help set off the log walls and other wood members in each room.

Kitchens and Bathrooms

Unless the log home you choose to rebuild has been modernized fairly recently, you will probably need to thoroughly transform the kitchen and bathrooms. In the typical older home, you will find a rather haphazard collection of counters, sinks, cabinets and other features in the kitchen. Similarly, the bathroom may be little more than a closet that was pressed into cramped service with a toilet, sink and tub when the plumbing moved indoors.

If the existing kitchen space is acceptable, but the entire room needs rebuilding, you may opt to install prefabricated cabinets, built-in range and other modern kitchen equipment rather than try to salvage what is already there. This saves time, if not money, and many custom cabinetmakers produce styles that are well-suited to log homes.

Perhaps the cabinets, counters and other kitchen fixtures currently in the house — or many of them — can be rebuilt or refinished. In many cases, these will have been painted, perhaps with several coats over the years, and you may prefer to strip off the paint and finish the wood naturally. This involves a lot of time and work, and a great deal of stripping solution if you must remove the paint from many surfaces.

Follow the same steps for both detachable parts — doors and drawers — and for built-in woodwork.

Here are the steps.

1. Remove the doors from the hinges and then re-move the hardware (knob pulls; leave hinges on doors). This is important to avoid leaving small patches on the edges of the door.

2. Lay the door or drawer down on several sheets of newspaper; or, if doing the woodwork, place newspapers along the floor. Always use rubber gloves. Brush on the varnish remover, making sure to cover all surfaces on the side facing up. Let sit about 10 minutes, and with a smooth motion scrape off the old varnish. It will peel off in clumps, but might re-quire two or three coats to get all the way down to the wood at all points. Turn the door over and do the second side.

3. Rub with solvent to get any remaining varnish out of grooves.

4. Sand firmly with fine sandpaper, until the wood has an even grain. (This is important; otherwise the stain may not take evenly.)

5. Apply stain with long, brushing movements using rags. Make sure the stain has been well stirred, and that you have allowed enough time for the solvent, used to wash down the wood, to evaporate. Make the first staining a "wet" layer — heavy and dark. Let sit about ten to fifteen minutes, and then wipe off with a soft absorbent cloth, again with even strokes. Then wait an hour. Apply a second coat, but not as heavy, working it until you get approximately the shade desired. Wipe again after ten minutes. If it still is not dark enough, apply a light final coat to darken with no excess to wipe off. Let sit 24 hours or more before applying lacquer or varnish.

6. To get a glossy finish, apply two or three coats of varnish or lacquer (follow directions on the can). To get a smooth, satiny finish, sand down the first coat after it has dried completely (fine sandpaper), and then apply a second coat; sand again once completely dry and hard (or just use "satin" varnish).

Commercial stripping solutions are costly. If you wish to save some money you can brew your own stripping compound. Mix two tablespoons of cornstarch in two quarts of water and stir thoroughly. Then, add half of a one-pound can of lye and stir constantly until the chemical reaction has stopped. If the material has not been stirred enough the lye will cook the cornstarch, and the result will be lumps instead of smooth, thick liquid.

Depending on the thickness of the paint (or old varnish), you'll need to apply this rather mild stripping solution four times or more, washing it off completely with water each time. Once the wood has been completely cleaned, it can be given a light coat of stain and either varnished or left unvarnished, for a handsome natural appearance.

Bathrooms, like kitchens, may require anything from a complete rebuilding to a thorough cleaning and sprucing up. Most older log cabins were not built with indoor plumbing originally. The bathroom, in most cases, will have a decided "afterthought" appearance.

If you are doing an extensive remodeling job, or reassembling a log house that has been moved from another location, you may want to plan your bathroom from scratch. Should you decide to make an addition to the original house, perhaps a shed-roofed lean-to on one end, you may want to house the kitchen and bathroom in this new section. In this way, you can allow

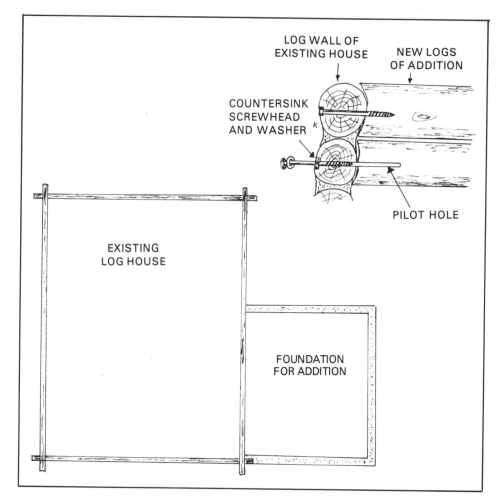

LOG WALL OF
EXISTING HOUSE

NEW LOGS
OF ADDITION

COUNTERSINK
SCREWHEAD
AND WASHER *k*

PILOT HOLE

Additions to existing log houses should be placed on solid foundations and securely anchored to the original building. Sketch shows how to anchor new logs of approximately the same size to log walls of an existing structure.

EXISTING
LOG HOUSE

FOUNDATION
FOR ADDITION

more space for fixtures and appliances, apply tile or other washable wall coverings, and come up with a kitchen and bath facility that better meets the needs of your family.

If the current bathroom space is ample, but the fixtures need replacing, consider using vanity lavatories and combination shower-tub units in your remodeling. These units cost more initially, but they can cover up a lot of what may be "problem area" walls in older bathrooms.

Utilities

Until you have thoroughly inspected the older house that you hope to recycle, it's hard to guess as to how extensive the repairs for the electrical wiring and the plumbing will be.

The wiring may be a series of electrical runs strung about in an extension-cord fashion to power bar bulb lights and to feed exposed outlet boxes. In one way, you'll have fewer problems with re-wiring a log house than with an old frame house: It is doubtful that any

wiring will be run inside the walls. Refer to Chapter 12 for various ways to install electrical wiring.

In most cases, you probably *will* need to replace the entire electrical system, including the service panel. Build in ample capacity in the entrance cable, service panel and wiring circuits — not only to handle current power demands but to allow for expanded needs later on.

The plumbing in an older house, like the electrical wiring, probably will need extensive overhauling. If you are rebuilding or reassembling a log structure, it is logical to renew the water and sewer service piping as the work progresses. Even in a house that requires only remodeling, you probably will want to replace or add on to the plumbing for new fixtures. You may also need to install a new septic tank system; drill a new well or drill an existing well deeper to provide a water volume needed for laundry equipment, or dishwashers, (see chapter 12).

You will want to keep potential problems and costs (in both time and dollars) in mind as you inspect a potentially renewable older log home. You are volunteering for a lot of hard work when you undertake to recycle an old house, at best. Make sure that the existing material is truly worth salvaging before you start.

Two Success Stories.

Here are examples of how other owners of older log buildings have rebuilt and restored them into sound dwellings.

The Wards' 160 Year-Old New Home

The planning is the fun part of redoing an older log home; the actual remodeling is just plain hard work. Jack and Martha Ward, of Montevallo, Alabama, can testify to that fact.

"We had a crew working on the house for six months," said Martha Ward. "We probably could have built an entire subdivision with the work we put into this one house."

Mrs. Ward was only partly kidding as she recalled the work that went into the farmhouse they recently remodeled. The structure was built about 1820, as far as Mrs. Ward has been able to determine.

The historic Balch House in northwest Alabama is built of yellow poplar, oak and yew logs cut from the site in 1880. It has been restored at the Burritt Museum, near Huntsville, Alabama. This house is of the same general style as the one rebuilt by Jack and Martha Ward (Photo Courtesy Burritt Museum)

"The house stands on what was a land grant to Richard Crowson, dated June 2, 1823, and signed by President James Monroe," said Mrs. Ward. "Records indicate that the house was built before the land grant was made."

When the Wards bought the property in 1973, they at first thought the building was a rather conventional old farmhouse that might be remodeled into a livable home.

"In fact, we didn't realize until later that the house was built of logs," she said. "The logs were covered with siding on the outside and sheetrock on the inside. It wasn't until we started examining the structural condition of the house that we discovered the log walls."

And what logs they are! Squared heartwood pine logs, each six inches thick and up to 18 inches wide — and some of them more than 40 feet long. Alabama grew spectacular timber back then.

The house contained four rooms, each 18-by-18 feet square — two upstairs and two down, with a 10-foot-wide dogtrot in the center of the house. Each room had a fireplace built of handmade brick. When they discovered what they had in the old house, and after Mrs. Ward had probed into the history of the farm and the building, the Wards hired the architectural firm of Kidd, Wheeler and Prosser to help them plan the restoration.

"Two layers of siding came off the outside; the sheetrock had to be taken off the inside of the walls," continued Mrs. Ward. "We cleaned the logs, inside and out, with an electric wire brush, then coated them with a sealer. We replaced the chinking between the logs with mortar."

Framed additions had been made to the house over the years, in sort of peicemeal expansion. Most of this was torn down. A shed-roofed addition on the back of the house was retained; it is now the Wards' kitchen.

The Wards took down the four fireplaces and their chimneys, brick by brick, and rebuilt three of the four with the same bricks. They replaced the roof, also.

"The floors had been replaced earlier and only needed refinishing," said Mrs. Ward. "We also put in central heating and air-conditioning, but hid as much of it as possible, so the house would retain its character."

An upstairs loft was remodeled into two bedrooms and a bath. When the Wards tore away the wall covering upstairs, they found gunports in the log walls. The original stairway in the living room was refinished, and the Wards built a new stairway in the dogtrot area as well. What started out as a remodeling job on an old farmhouse turned out to be the complete renovation of one of the oldest homes in the state. The Wards' home

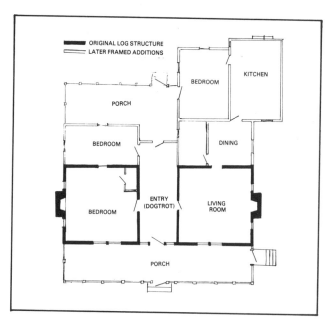

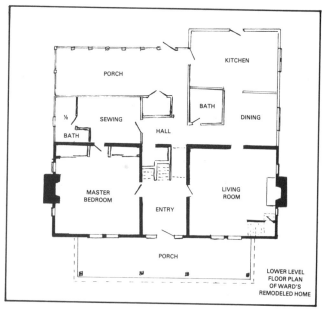

Through the years, the Ward home was added on to in rather piecemeal fashion. This is the lower level floor plan when the Wards bought the property in the early 1970's.

Part of the add-on structure was retained in the remodeled plan of Ward's home, to house kitchen, dining room, bath and sewing room. A new stairway was built in the dog-trot area, the front porch was rebuilt and three of the four original fireplaces were rebuilt from the original bricks.

The Ward's House

Don't overlook old barns, smokehouses and other buildings as a source of recycle-able logs.
(Courtesy Burritt Museum)

has now been listed in the Alabama Register of Landmarks and Heritage.

But Jack and Martha Ward's home is not merely another museum house. It is a full-time family residence with historical ties to a time before Alabama was even admitted as a state.

Dismantling and Restoring

A few years back Houston architect Carroll Tharp and his wife bought a 20-foot-square log house built in the mid-1850's; they carefully dismantled the structure, hauled it more than 100 miles and rebuilt it. The house, called the "Crane House," had eight-foot porches at the front and rear, and is one of the older homes in that section of Texas.

Tharp, who serves on the National Preservation subcommittee of the American Institute of Architects, has a long-time interest in restoring old buildings. He decided to move the Crane House to his property and rebuild it as nearly to the original construction as possible.

Tharp's first step was to number every part of the building, and make photos and sketches to show how all pieces fit together. The logs were joined at corners with dovetail notches that had to be fitted back together in exactly the right sequence.

The building was dismantled, piece by piece. The logs and other parts were loaded onto a truck. A few pieces of the dovetail corners came off during this operation; Tharp numbered them along with the logs they belonged to and later epoxied them back into their correct positions.

After hauling the building 100 miles, the Tharps discovered that their semi-trailer truck could not negotiate the crooked country road and narrow bridge to their property. The logs had to be unloaded nearly a half-mile away. Each log was dragged behind the family car the 2,000 feet or so to the building site. The Tharps used a rubber-tired trailer skid arrangement to hold one end of the log off the ground as it was being dragged.

After moving all the pieces to the building site in this manner, all parts were set up on blocks and coated with two coats of penta preservative. The Tharps removed all the decayed wood and filled the resulting cavities with a mixture of epoxy and sawdust. Some of the logs, rafters and beams required extensive surgery, Tharp said, and were rebuilt with the epoxy-sawdust mixture and new wood. The newly dressed wood was lightly stained to match the original color of the members repaired.

Three of the original 48 logs had to be replaced completely. These new logs were finished so they

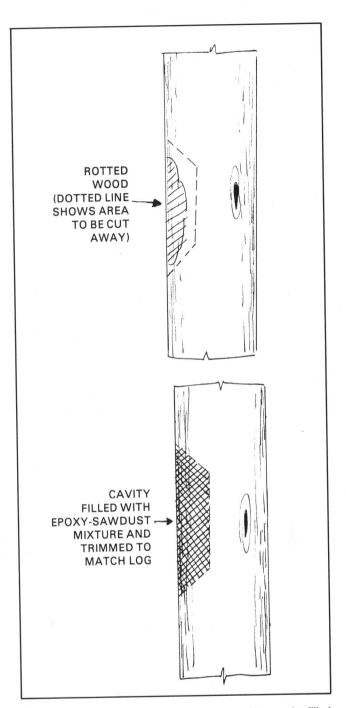

ROTTED WOOD (DOTTED LINE SHOWS AREA TO BE CUT AWAY)

CAVITY FILLED WITH EPOXY-SAWDUST MIXTURE AND TRIMMED TO MATCH LOG

Decayed wood can be cut away, and the resulting cavity filled with a mixture of industrial-grade epoxy and sawdust. The mixture should be about the consistency of thick oatmeal when applied, and can be thickened by adding more sawdust.

resembled the axe marks on the original logs and stained to match the color of the wood. The logs were raised into position with a block-and-tackle by roping the logs up sloping poles propped against lower logs.

"My investigations of old log houses have shown that they most often deteriorate because of the rotting of wood pilings or shifting of the rock foundations supporting the sills," said Tharp. "The twelve-inch-square sill members under our house had rolled almost completely off the rock foundations, since the rocks were originally laid with nothing else under them."

When reassembling the house, Tharp placed it on large precast concrete pads. The original foundation stones were set into the concrete in their original positions, however, and the sill logs rested directly on these stones. The soil around each pier was treated with Chlordane insecticide.

Many of the pole rafters of the old building had to be replaced. Tharp cut down some pine saplings on his property, peeled them and made a special jig so the end cuts matched the old pole rafters. These poles then were placed in position and stained to match the color of the salvaged rafters. The material used to box in the gables had originally been long-leaf yellow pine slabs. There was no way to duplicate them, so Tharp used six-inch-wide cypress siding.

The original roof had been made of 24-inch-long split cypress singles. This, too, proved to be a material long out of stock. Tharp replaced the roof with 24-inch red cedar shingles, lapped to duplicate the original roof.

The chimney, originally of mud and sticks, was rebuilt of brick.

"We made these and a few other compromises, but tried to remain true to history insofar as it was practical in rebuilding the house," said Tharp. "I concealed a lightning protection system in the masonry work of the chimney and used a diagonal subfloor with insulation between it and the old original wood flooring." On cold winter nights, there is little doubt in Tharp's mind as to the merits of this latter compromise.

"As for the rest of the building, we have strictly followed tradition," continued Tharp. "The doors are well over a hundred years old and were salvaged from another old building."

The Tharps worked two and a half years at their restoration project. Then more recently, putting their experience to work again, they moved and started restoring an even older log house. This one, however, only had to be hauled 40 miles.

You may not be able to acquire a log house with the history of those restored by the Tharps and Wards. And you may not want to adhere as rigidly to historical details of construction as these rebuilders did.

But the point made is this: older log homes exist; a great many of them have recycling potential, and some of them with a great deal of history enclosed within their walls. They *can* be rebuilt or remodeled into modern, comfortable dwellings. And they can be restored with historical integrity if the rebuilder is willing to invest the time and work.

If you elect to go the recycling route, your remodeling or rebuilding project will be the first of exactly its kind... ever. And the home that results will be the only one of its kind, too.

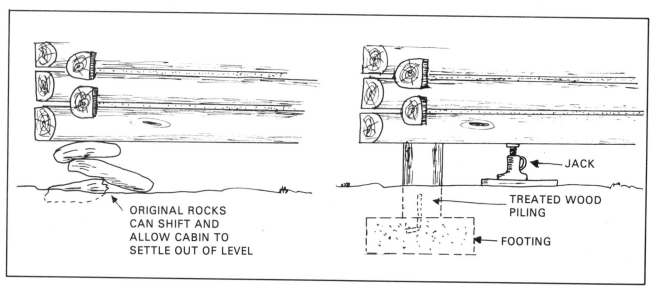

Sliding rocks, or rotting wood pilings, let older log homes sag and settle out of level. The house can be re-leveled with heavy jacks, and new foundations or piers installed on footings placed below frost line.

10.

DOORS AND WINDOWS ALSO DECKS, PORCHES AND STAIRS

Details of construction for such features as doors, windows, decks, porches and stairs are similar, whether you are building from scratch, from precut logs, or rebuilding an existing log structure. That is why we have grouped these features together rather than discuss them separately in previous chapters.

Stairways should be framed out as floors are framed, of course. You will want to make provision for basement stair openings in the first-floor framing. Main stair openings will be framed into the second-floor system, whether you use conventional lumber for joists or use log joists and girders.

Porch and deck framing, ideally, should also be incorporated in the framing for the main part of the house. These features appear less of an "afterthought" when planned into the basic house design.

Door and Window Installation

You will get a tighter, more weatherproof fit around doors and windows if you install them as an integral part of the wall, as logs are placed (mentioned in Chapter 7).

There are several ways to do this: You can either build roughed-in casings to be fitted in the wall, or use complete window-and-sash units (also door-and-frame units) from lumberyards, log home companies or other precut home manufacturers. If you are building a precut home, door and window installation will be an integral part of the design.

If you buy door and window units from a log home company (and several companies sell these and other components separately from kits) to be installed in a house you are building from scratch, the frame will be fitted with whatever features the particular company uses to integrate them into the wall — splines, mortise-and-tenon or other method. This means you will need to shape the abutting ends of logs to accommodate the interlocking feature used in the window or door.

Rough-in casings should be built of heavier material than you would normally use for frame construction. Two-inch dimensional lumber is best, with the frames squared and braced firmly.

Doors or door frames usually are set directly on the subfloor, to serve as a form for the logs that butt on both sides of the opening. Windows will be set into the wall at a predetermined height. If you are building from a kit, one course of logs will be marked as sills for windows. If you are using squared logs in from-scratch construction, a little planning can let you install windows or frames on one course of logs in similar fashion. If your logs are of uneven thickness, some notching and cutting will probably be necessary to get window sills at a uniform height.

Allow for Log Movement

All logs settle somewhat, after being laid up in the wall, and allowance for settling and shrinkage must be made when door and window frames are fastened to the walls. You'll want to leave some head-space at the top of openings to allow for movement of the logs. Usually, 3/4 inch to one inch of space is sufficient, unless logs are green when laid up. The "settling allowance" gap left between the top of the frame and the log above should be filled with insulation and then covered (sketch on p. 72 in Chapter 7 shows one method). If your roof has an overhang of two-feet or more, you may not need the metal flashing or drip-cap. The accompanying sketch shows how to use trim over the gap.

When fastening door and window frames to the ends of abutting logs you should again take into account the settling and movement of the logs. The sides of the frames should not be rigidly attached to the logs; as logs settle, the frame and window (or door) may bind.

One way to handle this is to make a one-inch vertical slot in the frame. Drive a nail through the slot

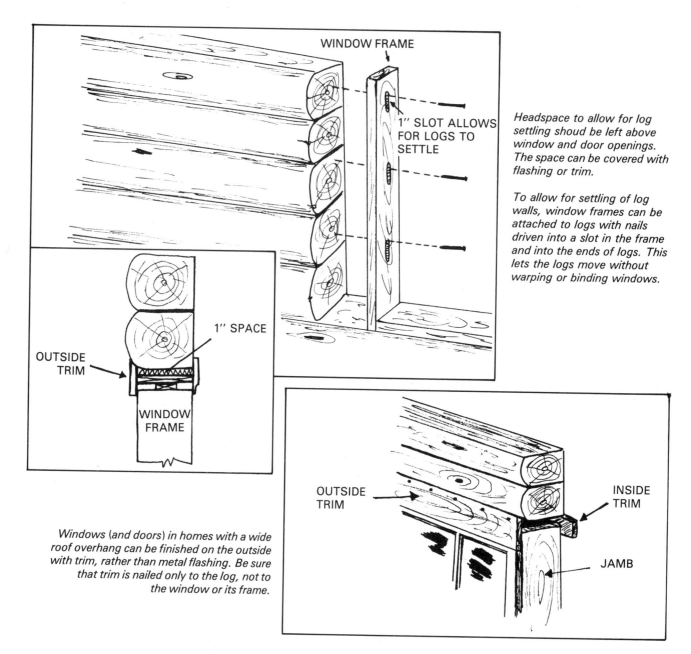

WINDOW FRAME

1" SLOT ALLOWS FOR LOGS TO SETTLE

Headspace to allow for log settling shoud be left above window and door openings. The space can be covered with flashing or trim.

To allow for settling of log walls, window frames can be attached to logs with nails driven into a slot in the frame and into the ends of logs. This lets the logs move without warping or binding windows.

OUTSIDE TRIM

1" SPACE

WINDOW FRAME

OUTSIDE TRIM

INSIDE TRIM

JAMB

Windows (and doors) in homes with a wide roof overhang can be finished on the outside with trim, rather than metal flashing. Be sure that trim is nailed only to the log, not to the window or its frame.

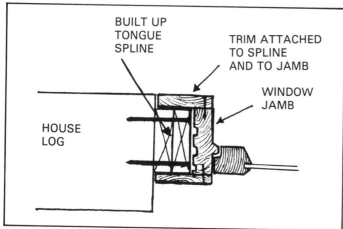

BUILT UP TONGUE SPLINE

TRIM ATTACHED TO SPLINE AND TO JAMB

WINDOW JAMB

HOUSE LOG

A tongue-type spline can be nailed to log ends, which fits snugly inside trim nailed to each side of the window or door casing. This lets the log move without binding the window.

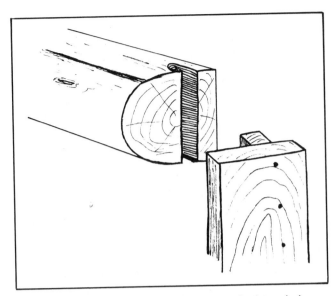

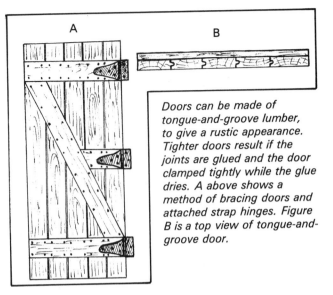

Another method is when the spline is attached to window or door casings, with a corresponding notch cut into the end of the log. A hole bored through the log, and the notch finished wilth a chisel works—but it takes a lot of boring and chiseling.

near the top, into the end of the log. However, do not draw the nail up tight, so the log can move downward without putting pressure on the window or door frame. You may want to attach the frame to several logs for support, using slots each time so logs can move without warping window or door frames.

Shown are alternate methods of attaching frames to the logs. Have these joining members fit snugly, but not tight enough to bind the frames if logs should move slightly.

Note. Do not use rigid insulation in the opening above the window frame. This defeats the purpose of leaving the gap in the first place.

Doors

As mentioned previously, you can buy pre-assembled door-and-frame units for both exterior and interior doors. Or, you can make your own to suit the overall appearance of your home.

Two-inch tongue-and-groove lumber with "Z" braces let in will give a rustic-looking door. Still more rustic, but more trouble, are doors made of sawmill slabs taken off as logs are sawed. The slabs can be faced for a tight fit and joined together to make a door.

Porches

An attached porch in keeping with the house design adds to the overall pleasing appearance of a

Doors can be made of tongue-and-groove lumber, to give a rustic appearance. Tighter doors result if the joints are glued and the door clamped tightly while the glue dries. A above shows a method of bracing doors and attached strap hinges. Figure B is a top view of tongue-and-groove door.

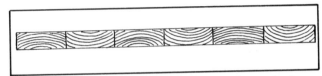

Doors made of planks butted together can be used, also. Alternate end grains of the planks, so that any cupping is not all in the same direction.

Doors of sawmill slabs are harder to build. The edges of the slabs should be finished for a tight fit, and cross braces should be let in for strength.

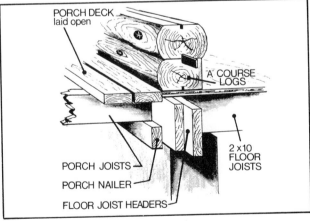

Porch framing should be incorporated with framing for the main part of the house. In pre-cut kit log homes, porches (if included) are installed as the house goes up. (Courtesy of Vermont Log Builders, Inc.)

home. The connections of the porch framing members to the main house should be by sills, joists and roof sheathing. The porch rafters, joists and studs should be securely attached to the house framing.

You may want the porch roof to continue the slope of the house roof itself. Or, the overhang at the gable can be extended to partially shelter the porch. If head-room will be short on the porch, you may want to make just enough pitch to the porch roof to provide good drainage.

Floors on open porches, whether of wood or concrete, should have a slight slope away from the house for drainage. Floor framing for wood porches should be at least 18 inches above the ground. Wood used for finish porch floors should have good decay resistance and be free of splintering and warping. Species commonly used are cypress, cedar and redwood. Treat material with a preservative where moisture conditions might cause problems.

Supports for enclosed porches usually consist of fully framed stud walls. Studs on 24-inch centers, rather than 16-inch centers as in partitions in the house, are ample support for most porches. Double the studs at openings and corners.

In open, or partially open porches, however, solid or built-up poles, posts or columns are used. You can use straight, peeled and trimmed poles for open porches. Or, for a more finished appearance, as with a partially enclosed porch, columns can be made of doubled 2X4's, which are covered with a 1X4 casing on two opposite sides and by 1X6's on the other sides.

Slats or grillwork used around an open crawl space under the porch should be made with a removable section for access to areas where termites may be present. Use a vapor barrier of plastic or roofing felt over the ground under a closed-in porch. A fully enclosed crawl space should be vented or have an opening into the basement.

Decks

Outdoor living is popular with most American families; even people living in northerly states spend a lot of time outdoors in warmer weather. A wood deck can be a seasonal living room, adding space to a home at modest cost. On steep hillside sites, a deck may be the best way to provide a comfortable, accessible outdoor area near the house.

Location

Most decks are attached to the house, for access and part of their support. As with porches, it is an

High-level decks, perhaps off upstairs bedrooms, offer outdoor areas with privacy.

advantage if the design of a deck can be incorporated into the design of the house. The deck can be designed as an outdoor extension of a kitchen or dining room, perhaps with access through sliding doors. Or a high deck — above a porch or lower level deck — can provide accessible outdoor areas to both floors of a two-story house.

Deciding where a deck will be located goes a long way toward determining what kind of deck to build. The location should take into account prevailing winds, as well as sunny and shaded areas during different times of the day. A deck built on the east side of the house will be shaded for evening cook-outs and parties. A high-level deck, built off a south-facing upstairs bedroom, catches late-evening breezes after the sun has set in summer. It also offers more privacy than exposed low decks. This may not be a major factor for log home dwellers in the country, with no close-at-hand neighbors or passing traffic. But privacy often comes at a premium in towns and subdivisions.

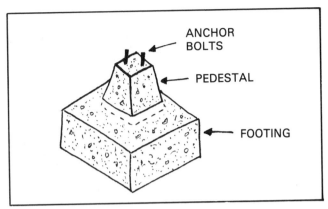

Footing and pedestal underpinnings provide good support for deck posts. The pedestal should extend six inches or above grade:

Deck posts should be bolted or pinned to pedestals. Use a layer of tar paper or roofing, pasted down with asphalt cement, under the post.

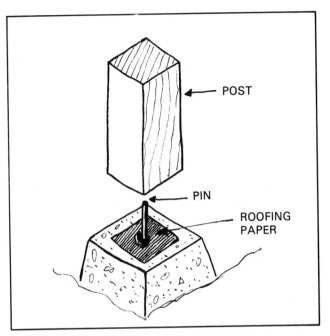

Construction Pointers

Some kind of footing should be used to support the posts or poles which transfer the deck loads to the ground; a concrete footing is usually most satisfactory. The footing should be placed below the frost line and below any fill dirt. Footings should be at least 12-by-12 inches, by eight inches thick. Where poles or posts will be spaced more than six feet apart, a footing 20 inches square by 10 inches thick should be used.

It is best to put the posts or poles that will support the deck above ground level. A pedestal-type footing like that sketched here, which extends at least six inches above the ground surface, is a good underpinning for most decks. Use non-staining, rustless fastenings in deck construction. Bolts hold more securely than nails. Where posts must be used below grade, they should be pressure-treated with a preservative.

Low wood decks over fairly level ground can be supported on concrete piers or short sections of logs for posts. It is important that the soil slope away from the area under low-level decks, for good water drainage and moisture control.

Decks commonly are floored with spaced planking, preferably of decay-resistant, non-splintering wood. Some are floored with plywood that is sealed with an epoxy coating or other waterproof treatment.

Ideally, wood for exposed decks should be pressure-treated with a preservative. But regular applications of a preservative that is brushed or sprayed on will add many years of life to wood exposed to the weather. When treating the wood, give a double dose to joints and the exposed grain ends of framing members.

Stairs

Generally, stairways are constructed of materials and designs that complement the overall construction of the house. Rough-sawed planks or half-log open stairs lend a rustic appearance, as do railings and balusters made of peeled poles. Or for a home finished in more contemporary style stairs can be enclosed and perhaps carpeted.

Openings in the floor for stairways are framed out during construction of the floor system. The long dimension of the stairway can be either parallel or at right angles to the joists. However, it is easier to frame a stairway opening with its length parallel to the joists. This is also the stronger construction, unless some support is placed beneath joists headed at right angles to the run of the stairs. Stairs in split-level houses may *have* to be framed at right angles to the joists.

Rough openings for the main stairway are usually 10 feet long, depending on the height of the second floor above the main floor. Widths should be three feet or more. For basement stairs, a rough opening may be about nine feet, six inches long by 32 inches wide. The width of 32 inches is two joist spaces.

The width of main stairs should be at least two feet, eight inches, inside any handrails. When the

107

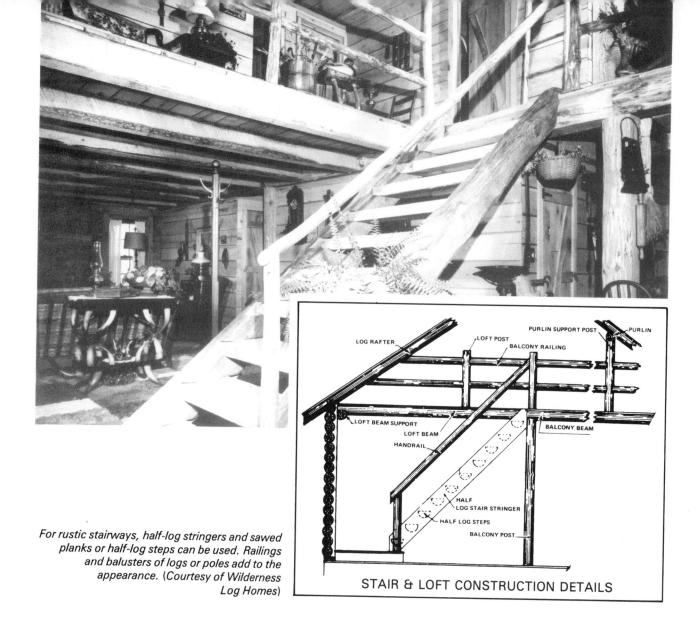

For rustic stairways, half-log stringers and sawed planks or half-log steps can be used. Railings and balusters of logs or poles add to the appearance. (Courtesy of Wilderness Log Homes)

STAIR & LOFT CONSTRUCTION DETAILS

stairway runs between two walls some stairs are designed with a distance of three feet, six inches between the centerlines of sidewalls. This results in a net width of about three feet. Split-level entrance stairs are commonly wider; up to four feet or more.

Step Proportions

There's a definite relationship between the height of the riser (the vertical step-up) and the width (depth) of the tread (the horizontal run) in a stair. Have you ever noticed that steps with shorter risers usually have deeper, wider treads, and vice versa? There's a good, time-tested reason for this. If the combination of rise and run is too great, there is strain on the leg muscles — and maybe on the heart. In a stair with a high riser, or vertical distance, the legs are lifting the body's weight more nearly vertically. The feet cannot reach a great forward, horizontal distance and still give the legs the leverage they need to pull the body up the stairs.

The reverse is nearly as awkward. Stairs with short risers are an easier climb — more nearly like walking on level surfaces — and the tendency is to take a longer forward step. If the short riser is accompanied by a narrow tread, the climber kicks his toe against the riser with each step, and must make a conscious effort to take small steps.

The relation of riser-to-tread area influences walking down stairs as well as climbing up, and a stair that is designed out of proportion can be unsafe.

Here is a rule of thumb for figuring the relation between the height of the riser and the width of the tread: the tread width multiplied by the riser height, in inches, should range from 72 to 75. For example, a riser height of 7½ inches should be matched with a net tread width of 10 inches (7½ X 10 = 75).

Of course, this formula can be carried to ridiculous extremes. You would not build stairs with 25-inch risers and three-inch treads, although that combination totals 75. Experience shows that a riser from 7½ to eight inches high, with the appropriate tread width, combines both safety and comfort.

To lay out a stair, first measure the total rise (vertical distance) from the finished floor at the foot of the stairs to the finished floor at the top of the stairs. If finished flooring has not been laid yet (and it usually will not be when you build the stairway), include the thickness of the floor material that will be used in the measurement.

Let's suppose the rise of your stairway measures eight feet, 10½ inches. That includes: eight feet from the main floor to the bottom of the ceiling joists, 9½

inches for the joists, 5/8-inch for the subfloor in the second story, and 5/8-inch for the finished floor — or a total of 106¼ inches.

Since that distance is to be divided into stair risers of equal height, the first computation is to find what riser height divides equally into 106¼ inches. For example, to get this distance divided exactly into 14 equal units, you have to carry it out to 64ths of an inch, which is narrower than a carpenter's pencil mark. The closest practical division is 13 risers each 7-5/8 inches high, plus one rise of about 7-3/8 inches. This works out well because the last step at the top of the stairs will

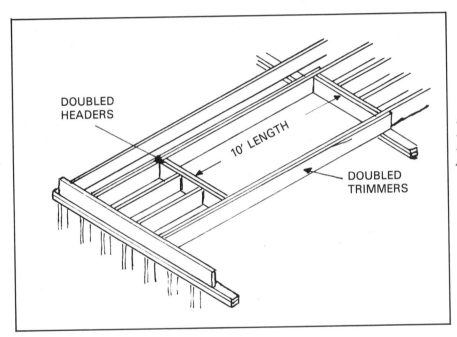

DOUBLED HEADERS

10' LENGTH

DOUBLED TRIMMERS

If possible, stair openings should be framed with the length parallel to the direction joists are laid.

Steps nailed on top of cleats can be used for main stairways, basement stairs or steps up to a porch or deck. Steps placed to end at ground level should be anchored to a concrete pad. You can use an angle iron, bolted to the steps and to the concrete pad.

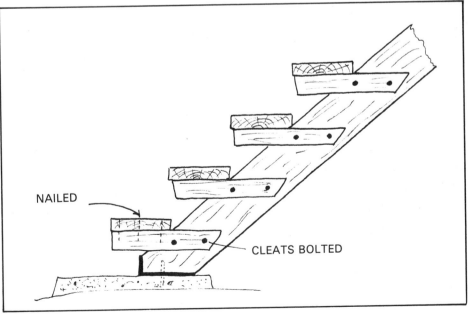

NAILED

CLEATS BOLTED

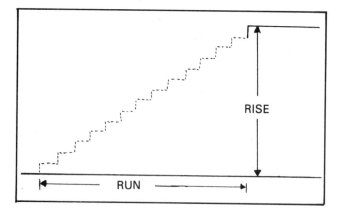

To lay out a stair, start by measuring the total rise. Don't forget to allow for the thickness of floor materials to be installed later.

be onto the floor of the second story. When the stair carriage has been marked and cut it will be attached to the joist or header 7-3/8 inches below the second-story floor level.

Since the top step will be onto the upstairs floor, and the joist or header will be the riser for that step, we can proceed to lay out the other 13 equal steps, each 7-5/8 inches high, on the stair carriage or stringer. The treads will be 9-3/4 inches deep, which makes the total rise-and-run for each riser and tread combination fall within the "72 to 75" thumbrule previously outlined. The total horizontal run (depth front to back) of the stairway will be about 124 inches (13 X 9-3/4 inches).

The stair carriage can be of any material — whole logs, half logs, slabs, dimension lumber. The procedure for laying out stairs is the same; however, round logs are somewhat more difficult to mark and cut accurately.

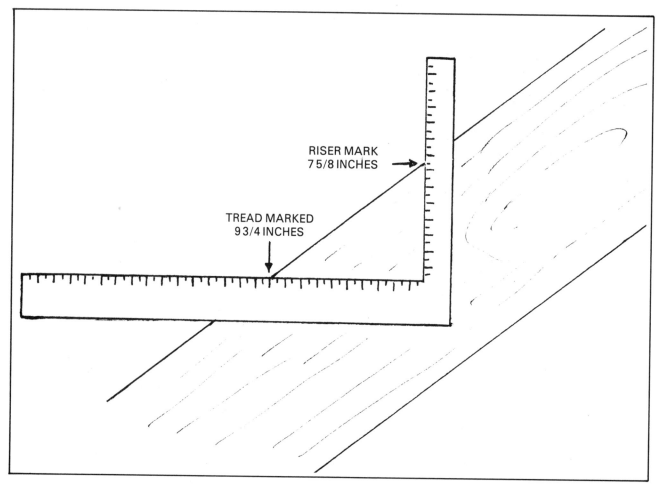

RISER MARK
7 5/8 INCHES

TREAD MARKED
9 3/4 INCHES

To mark stair treads and risers with a framing square, place the square so that the tread width is on the body and the riser height is on the tongue of the square. Mark the 90-degree angle thus made.

For the sake of illustration we will show a stair carriage made from 2X12 stock. Start at one end of the 2X12 and place the tongue of a framing square so that the 7-5/8-inch mark on the square aligns with the edge of the board. Hold the tongue of the square at this point and swivel the square so that the 9-3/4-inch mark on the body of the square also aligns with the edge of the board. Mark the right angle made. Now, move the square so that 9-3/4 inches on the body aligns with the top mark, and so that 7-5/8 inches on the tongue of the square aligns with the edge of the board beyond. Mark the angle, and repeat this procedure until all 13 risers and treads have been marked.

At the last corner of the last 90-degree angle marked, which represents the 13th tread at the top of the stairway, mark the end of the stringer so that it will be cut to rest flush against the joist or header. This cut

For enclosed stairways, a finish stringer (a sort of support frame for the stairs) can be installed before the notched stair carriage is put in place. Then, treads and risers are cut to fit tightly between the stringers and nailed to the carriage with finishing nails. (Drawing Courtesy UDSA Forest Service)

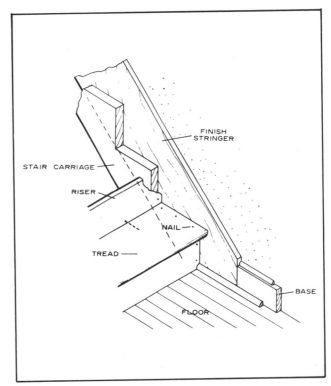

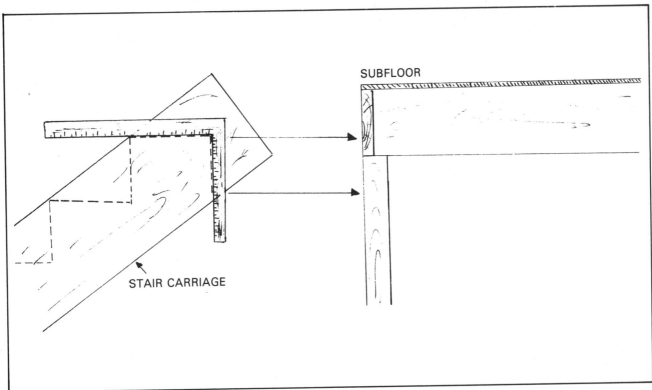

The final cut at the top of the stair should be made plumb, so that the stair carriage fits flush against the wall, with the top stair tread the "proper" distance below the subfloor level.

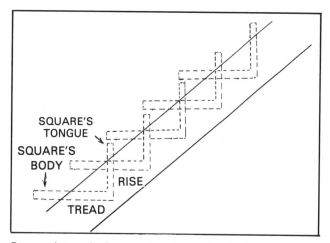

SQUARE'S
TONGUE

SQUARE'S
BODY

RISE

TREAD

Repeat the marks for each tread and riser 13 times, carefully aligning the framing square each time.

is made at right angles to the mark for the tread, but in the other direction than if you were laying out another riser, so that the mark extends to the opposite edge of the stringer.

A horizontal cut will need to be marked at the bottom of the stringer, too, where the piece rests flush against the floor.

By marking carefully, you can use the first stringer (after the treads and risers have been cut out) to mark the cuts for the second (and third, if you will be laying wider stairs that need support in the middle of the span) stringer.

Main stairway components (treads and risers) should be made of oak, birch, maple or similar long-wearing hardwoods, unless the stair is to be covered with carpeting or other material. A hardwood tread with a softwood riser can be combined for economy and easier working. Treads and risers for basement stairways can be made of Douglas fir, southern pine or similar medium-hardness woods.

11.

FIREPLACES AND CHIMNEYS

A log house without a fireplace seems incomplete, and a log house with a stone fireplace and chimney is even better. For best results, both should be planned at the same time and with equal care.

There are any number of usable designs for fireplaces, but a massive fireplace and chimney of stone seems to set off a log home especially well.

You will want to give a great deal of thought about where you will locate the fireplace — or fireplaces — as well as how large it will be and of what design. Plan carefully. The fireplace should harmonize in design and proportion with the room in which it is built, but must not sacrifice safety and function for appearance. A small room seems overwhelmed by too large a fireplace, just as too small a fireplace may lose some of its impact in a room that is too large or that has pretentious furnishings.

A traditional old-style masonry fireplace is great for atmosphere — and for raising fuel bills. While the fire is crackling in the fireplace, it draws heated air up the chimney and cold air from outside into the house. The result can be a net heat *loss,* even with the fireplace going full blast, when the inside-outside temperature difference is more than 30 degrees F. The fire may heat the immediate area around the fireplace by radiant heat, but it can cool the rest of the house by drafting warm air through the flue. That's one reason a metal fireplace unit, such as a *Heatilator* or *Heatform,* with a tight-closing damper and combustion-air intakes from outside the house, can add tremendously to the efficiency of a fireplace.

For several other reasons, you should seriously consider using a metal heat-circulating fireplace, which forms the main outline of the opening and a framework that can be covered with brick or stone masonry. The appearance — inside and outside the house — of such a fireplace need not be substantially different from a fireplace built outright from masonry.

For one thing, these prefabricated metal fireplaces are designed with the correct ratio of width, depth,

The fireplace exterior should suit the rest of the masonry in material and design; although stone and brick often are combined in complementary fashion—as in this home, with stone fireplace and retaining wall. (The "brick" on basement walls is actually a pattern formed in the concrete when poured.) (Courtesy of New England Log Homes, Inc.)

height, throat area and smoke shelf width to burn properly — so long as they are equipped with a flue of the proper size. A fireplace that does not "draw" right is a liability, rather than an asset.

Also, these fireplaces have tight-closing dampers built in, which helps prevent heat loss through the flue when the fireplace is not in use. They also have cold- and hot-air ducts that transmit heated air into the room, and can even be ducted to heat adjacent rooms. Blowers can be installed in the cold-air intakes, to push even more heated air into the rooms.

A duct coming from outside the house to the fireplace will provide most of the combustion air from outside, and not from heated air inside the heated house. A duct size of 28 square inches (six inches round or similar-sized rectangular duct) should run from the outside to inside tight-fitting glass doors on the fireplace. These glass doors should be kept closed, even when a fire is burning, to cut heat loss from the room. This conserves both the firewood consumed by the fireplace and the energy needed to heat the house by other methods.

Fireplaces on outside walls should have insulation between the fireplace and the outside masonry.

Fireplaces should be designed and sized for the room they will occupy. (Courtesy of Boyne Falls Log Homes, Inc.)

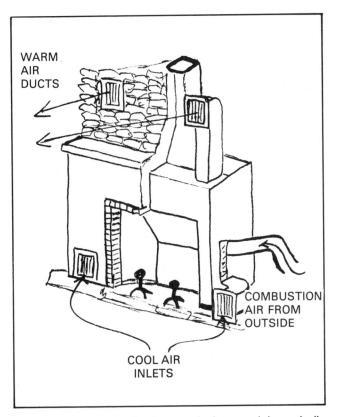

Heating efficiency of a fireplace can be increased dramatically by drawing combustion air from outside the house, and by ducting warmed air into adjacent rooms.

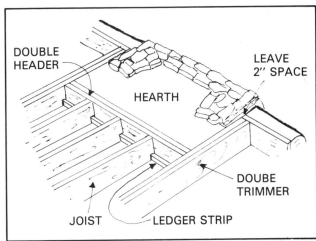

When framing around the fireplace opening, double joist headers and trimmers. Leave a two-inch space between the masonry and wood framing members at the side of the fireplace.

Since much of the heating value of a fireplace comes from heat radiated by the warmed masonry of the fireplace and chimney, you may want to give some thought to building the fireplace completely inside the house, rather than with the back of the fireplace and the chimney outside the wall. Fireplaces built completely inside do not add as much to the exterior appearance of the house, but are much more efficient as heating equipment.

If the fireplace is built on an outside wall, insulation should be placed between the back of the fireplace and the outside masonry to cut down on heat loss.

With a well-designed fireplace, ductwork and fans, and combustion air piped in from the outdoors, it is possible to heat a 2,000-square-foot house with a fireplace, with only some help from a furnace, heat pump or electric space heater in the very coldest weather. But unfortunately, most fireplaces built are not up to this kind of performance.

Footings and Foundations

A masonry fireplace is easily the heaviest part of a house. Along with its chimney, a stone or brick fireplace that spans most of one wall puts tons and tons of pressure on the footings and foundation.

Reinforced concrete footings are recommended. The footing must extend over a wide enough area to bear the weight without exceeding the load-bearing capacity of the soil. The fireplace footing should be formed and poured when the footings are made for the house foundation or basement wall.

The footing should extend below the frost line. Footings should extend at least six inches beyond the fireplace on all sides, and should be eight inches thick for one-story houses and 12 inches thick for two-story houses, or where the footing is made below the basement floor.

Insulated metal chimneys should extend three feet above the roof, and two feet above the highest point of the roof. These chimneys are fitted with fireproof fittings where they pass through the wall, ceiling and roof.

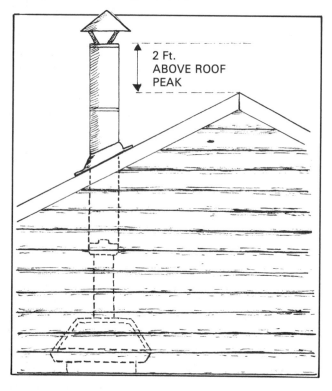

The sturdiest construction is to build up the fireplace foundation of solid masonry or poured concrete to the subfloor level. If the foundation and footing under it are to accommodate the width of the hearth in front of the fireplace, it provides a stronger construction. This way, a masonry hearth can be built straight up over the foundation, rather than corbelled out as is necessary in other methods.

If you will have more than one fireplace — perhaps a prefab stand-alone unit in another room or on another level — or wood-burning stove or furnace in addition to the fireplace, you will need flues to exhaust the smoke and fumes from these fixtures. If possible, these flues should be built into the main fireplace chimney, so that you need build only one chimney. However, no other fixture should be flued or vented into the fireplace flue itself.

Framing

The method of framing around a fireplace opening is similar to framing for a stairway, as outlined in Chapter 10. It should be taken care of when the subfloor is framed. Shown here is one method.

Fireplace and chimney footings and foundations should be made when the house foundation is poured. Note the ports in this corner fireplace foundation, which will allow outside air to be drawn into the firebox, when the fireplace is completed.

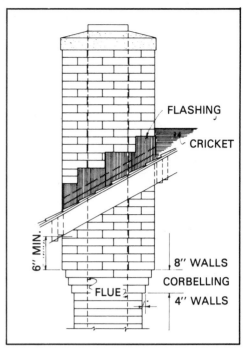

Metal flashing is inserted in mortar joints of the chimney, extending under the roofing shingles. In this photo, the metal flashing has been coated with asphalt roofing cement.

"Corbelling" is the technique of building out one or more courses of brick or stone, as pictured above. Masonry also can be corbelled out to form a fireplace hearth. (Sketch Courtesy USDA)

No wood members should be placed in contact with the chimney. Leave a two-inch space between the chimney and wooden girders and joists. Some log homes are built with the girder and joists bearing on the chimney. If this is the case, a supporting ledge should be corbelled out for the wooden member and insulating material installed between the wood and the masonry of the chimney.

Roof Connection

Where the chimney passes through the roof, provide a two-inch space between the wood members and the masonry. This gives some fire protection should mortar fall out of the joints between stones or bricks, and also permits expansion due to temperature changes and some slight movement during high winds.

Chimneys must be flashed, usually with metal shingles, to make the joint with the roof watertight. Corrosion-resistant metal, such as copper, zinc or aluminum, should be used. If you are using copper flashing, use copper nails. Otherwise, electro-galvanic action between dissimilar metals can cause copper to "fatigue" and become brittle.

The masonry at the top of the chimney should be finished off with a cement mortar cap. Mix a rich mortar of one part Portland cement with three parts of clean, fine sand. The cap should be finished with a straight or concave slope to shed water from the top of the

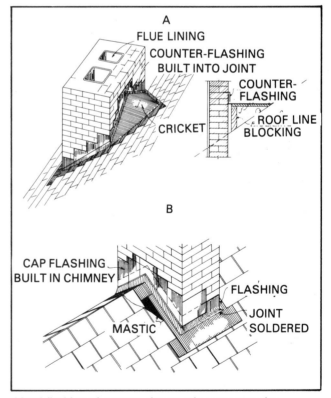

Metal flashing of copper, zinc or other noncorrosive metal should extend through mortar joints in the chimney and onto the roof sheeting, to be covered with roofing material. Drawing A, above, shows flashing installed and a "cricket" built to shed water around the chimney. Figure B shows how flashing is attached when the chimney is located on a roof ridge. (Drawings Courtesy USDA)

117

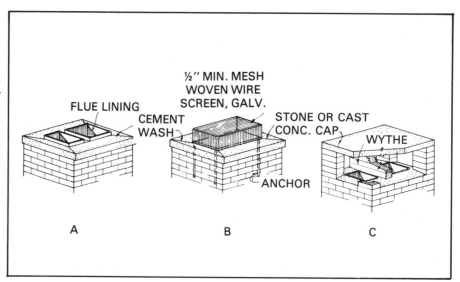

Flue linings should extend at least four inches above the top course of masonry, and finished with at least two inches of cement mortar. The mortar cap should have a concave slope to direct air currents upward and to drain water away from the flue. Figure A shows the cap on a two-flue chimney; figure B shows the cap with a screen spark arrester attached. As in figure C, a hood can be built to keep out rain.

chimney. The accompanying sketch shows how to build a chimney cap form that requires no braces or framing.

In most states and localities, it is illegal to support roof systems with any part of a chimney.

Flue Linings

Fireplace chimneys are often built without flue linings to cut costs, but lined flues are safer and more efficient since flues are subjected to rapid changes in temperature and the acids of combustion gases. Linings of vitrified (fired) fireclay are better able to withstand these stresses than are masonry and mortar.

Clay flue liners are made both rectangular and round. Round liners are more efficient, but rectangular ones adapt more readily to most masonry construction. The key is to use flue liners that are large enough. The below table lists recommended flue lining sizes (in inches) for various-sized fireplaces:

Flue liners are installed ahead of masonry work, so that the sections of liner butt tightly together and are bedded in mortar. This makes a smooth, tight joint. Liners usually start at the fireplace throat and extend four to six inches above the top of the chimney masonry.

Testing the Flue

A flue should be tested before being used. Ideally, the test should be made right away after the chimney is finished, so that any leaks can be patched before the chimney is enclosed by further construction.

Build a fire of paper, straw, leaves or other smoke-making material at the base of the flue. When the smoke rises thickly, block the top of the flue outlet with a wet blanket or burlap sack. Smoke that leaks through the masonry can be easily detected. Make sure you have adequate ventilation in the room while conducting this test.

Watch for leaks into adjoining flues in the chimney, through the walls of the flue or between the flue liner and the chimney wall. Use this same test for all flues in the chimney.

Prefabricated Stand-Alone Fireplaces

You can have a fireplace in practically any room of the house — or every room, if you wish — without going to a lot of trouble to pour footings, lay stone and all that. Simply install a prefabricated metal fireplace and insulated metal chimney.

While these factory-built units do not have the charm of a masonry fireplace, they are compact and easy to install. The free-standing models can be

Recommended Dimensions

Fireplace Width	Fireplace Height	Fireplace Depth	Rectangular Lining	Round Lining
24″	24″	16 - 18″	8½X8½″	10″
30	28	16 - 18	8½X13	10
36	30	16 - 18	8½X13	12
42	32	16 - 18	13X13	12
48	32	18 - 20	13X13	15
54	36	18 - 20	13X18	15
60	40	20 - 22	18X18	18

installed anywhere, some of them as closely as 12 inches to a wood wall. Some have insulated linings of firebrick or other refractory. They sell from $200 up, and the insulated metal chimney may cost nearly as much as the fireplace, if the chimney extends very high.

These fireplaces should sit on a pad and hearth of fireproof material — brick, ceramic tile, concrete, stone, etc. This hearth should cover the floor directly under the fireplace and extend at least six inches on both sides and to the rear, and about 18 inches in front.

You can connect one of these units to an unused flue, if you have one, or install double-walled insulated metal chimney sections, such as *Metalbestos,* which is

constructed of two layers of stainless steel with a layer of asbestos insulation between. The sections connect together with a bayonet-type mount that makes a smooth stainless-steel flue that can safely be used with wood-burning fireplaces and stoves, with no need for masonry work of any kind.

These chimneys can be run directly through the ceiling and roof over the fireplace, or can be attached to an outside wall. Insulated elbows and through-wall sections are built to be used with them. In either case, the chimney should extend at least three feet above the roof through which it passes, and at least two feet higher than the highest part of the roof.

Pre-fab "stand-alone" fireplaces can be placed anywhere, when used with a doubled-walled insulated flue.

12.

PLANNING THE UTILITIES

You've read it before in this book, in practically every chapter, but good planning can save time and money. That's as true of electrical wiring, plumbing, heating and air-conditioning as with any other phase of log home construction.

As you are laying out the house, the location of important services should be pinpointed in relation to the house itself — electrical meter pole, water well, sewer line and septic tank, fuel oil or LP-gas tank, etc. If you have these utilities located before the house excavation is made, the same digging machinery can probably make trenches for buried pipes, electrical cables and telephone lines. You can then run these service connections to the house, and have all the backfilling done at the same time.

The next element of planning is to arrange for the installation of services. It helps if you can give the electric company, the telephone company, etc., a date well ahead of the time you will need services. This lets the company schedule the installation work and can help get the services installed and connected when you need them.

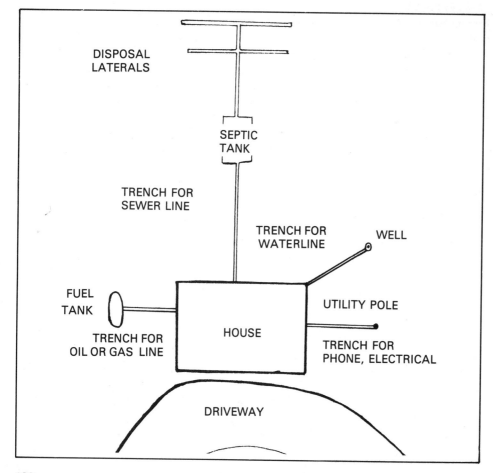

DISPOSAL LATERALS

SEPTIC TANK

TRENCH FOR SEWER LINE

TRENCH FOR WATERLINE

WELL

FUEL TANK

UTILITY POLE

TRENCH FOR OIL OR GAS LINE

HOUSE

TRENCH FOR PHONE, ELECTRICAL

DRIVEWAY

Layout planning can let the excavation work for house, septic tank and service lines be completed at the same time. Extra copies of the layout drawing can be made, to be given to power companies, telephone companies, well drillers, etc., in case the builder is absent when these services are installed.

Services During Construction

Even before the details of house wiring and plumbing are pinned down, you will want some services at the site. During construction, it is handy to have electrical service to operate saws, drills and other power tools. A telephone also is convenient during construction, as is a water supply. So, an early chore is to arrange for these services and to plan where they will be located in relation to the house itself. It helps to have several general layout sketches made up, such as the one shown. You can leave a copy with each service company, to be attached to the company work order. Then, if you must be away from the building site when the power company or well-driller arrives, they will know exactly where to locate these services.

Rural electric cooperatives generally place the last pole (the utility pole on which the meter may be located) about 100 feet from the house site. However, if you plan to run underground electrical service (and telephone service, since phone companies generally run lines in on electric poles) from the last pole to the house, you may want them to set the pole closer. This way, you will not have to buy and bury as much expensive underground electrical cable. Also, with the meter pole closer to the construction site, you will not need as much cord to run power tools during building.

The same thing applies to the water well (if you're having one drilled). Leave a layout drawing with the drilling company and also mark the location of the well at the site. There are some special considerations with locating a well for the family water supply. Your well should be located on a well-drained site, upslope from planned sewer lines and septic tank locations. The well, for obvious reasons, also should not be downhill from barns, corrals or poultry houses.

When the driller completes the well, he probably will draw a sample of the water to have it tested at a state-run laboratory. If he does not do this automatically, request that he send a sample for analysis and that a report of the water quality be sent to you. If a copy must be sent to the driller (as is the case in some states) request that a duplicate copy of the test results come to you. The test report will show coliform bacteria counts, the presence of organic chemicals — such as nitrates — and perhaps the mineral content of the water supply.

If you will be using a fuel oil or LP-gas furnace or water heater, you may not be in too much of a hurry to arrange for the tank and fuel lines to be installed. However, if you are building in cold weather, it is more comfortable to have space heaters to use after the building has been closed in. Different states have

When electrical, telephone and other services can be run underground, rather than overhead, the house and homesite blend better into surroundings, with fewer distractions. Electric meters, however, commonly are required to be placed outside. (Courtesy New England Log Homes, Inc.)

varying rules on the placement and hook-up of fuel tanks — minimum distance from the nearest building, that sort of thing. Your fuel service company man should know what regulations apply, but still it is one of those mind-easing bits of information you may want to learn for yourself.

Do-it-Yourself?

You may want to leave the details of house wiring and plumbing to professionals. If this is the case, it's a good idea to contact an electrician and plumber as soon as possible.

Even if you plan to do your own work, it's still a good idea to get in touch with professional tradesmen. They can be a lot of help in the planning stages, and can make follow-up checks of your work later on.

Don't be over-awed by the professional "mystique" that surrounds many of the construction trades. Electrical wiring is a fairly complicated undertaking, and can be dangerous if not properly done. Plumbing is not as potentially hazardous as electrical work, but it can result in nagging, persistent problems if not properly installed. However, a builder with moderate manual skills can do his own wiring and plumbing, safely and at a considerable savings compared with hiring the work done.

You may want to work more or less under the supervision of journeymen electricians and plumbers. They know what codes and regulations apply in your state and area, and can give you valuable advice at all stages of the game. Before you undertake your own wiring, check the building codes and insurance practices in your locality. In some states, the wiring must be done by a licensed electrician before utility companies will turn on the service.

In other areas, insurance rates are higher and coverage hard to get if wiring is not done by a professional. As with electrical service, many states and localities require that some aspects of plumbing be done by licensed professionals.

Usually, these rules are considered complied with if a licensed electrician and plumber are retained on a "consulting" basis, to inspect the final work before the building is closed in, circuits are energized and the water is turned on. (However, construction workers' unions in some areas forbid the approval of any work not done by union members. Again, check the rules before you start.)

Electrical Service

Planning your electrical service should take into account your electrical needs now, plus any expansion that might be made in the future. You will want to plan capacities on the high side. Heavier wiring and larger service panels cost more initially; but it is money saved in the long run, compared with beefing up capacity later on. It's not that much more costly to install 200-amp service than 100-amp service, and 200 amps should provide all the capacity you will ever need.

A valuable guide to all electrical work is the *National Electrical Code,* the standard of the National Board of Fire Underwriters. Your electrical supplier can provide a copy of this 400-pages-plus code.

An early decision to make is whether to bring electrical service into the house above ground or underground. If overhead service will be run, a weatherhead must be attached to the side or gable of the house, through which the power lines enter. Underground service, which usually enters a basement, costs a little more than overhead service, but is better protected from the weather and looks better.

The power lines enter the house and run to a distribution box. The various house circuits begin at this box. Virtually all electrical distribution today employs circuit breakers, rather than fuses, to protect the wiring and electrical connections from overloads.

Circuit breakers and the wiring in the circuits should be planned with the capacity to carry the lights, equipment and appliances used. As a rule of thumb, a 20-ampere circuit with No. 12 wire will serve a combined wattage of 2,500 watts. The table below lists some appliances and the amount of power they require:

Appliance	Watts
Electric blanket	150 to 200
Blender	250
Coffeemaker	600 to 1,000
Electric skillet	1,200 to 1,650
Clothes dryer (240V)	4,000 to 8,700
Home freezer	300 to 500
Furnace blower	800
Iron, hand	650 to 1,300
Motors: ¼ h.p.	300 to 400
½ h.p.	450 to 600
1 h.p.	950 to 1,000
Refrigerator	150 to 300
Range (240V)	8,000 to 16,000
Stereo hi-fi	100 to 400
Television	200 to 400
Washing machine	400 to 800
Water pump	300 to 1,000

Wiring

If you'll be wiring your own house, you may want to run the circuits, install outlet boxes, switches and lighting fixtures, then have a licensed electrician connect the circuits to the breaker panel. He can test each circuit before it is connected, to make sure that everything is wired properly.

Precut log homes usually have designed-in provisions for electrical wiring, either in the log walls themselves or in a special channel that will be covered by a baseboard or other trim. The kit and blueprints will indicate where and how wiring is to be run.

If you are building a log home from scratch, you will want to plan carefully the routes electrical wiring and other utilities are to take. Don't overlook other installation jobs that should be planned and installed at the same time, such as:

Thermostat wiring
  for furnace
TV antenna wiring;
  cable vision
Doorbells
Fans for fireplaces

Telephone wiring
Hi-fi speaker systems
Exhaust fans
Intercoms

Outlets installed in a baseboard that trims out the junction of floor and log wall. The baseboard conceals the wiring behind.

Log home companies usually make provisions for electrical service in the walls. Here, wiring is run in a pre-cut groove in the bottom log, which later is covered by a baseboard. (Courtesy of Authentic Homes Corp.)

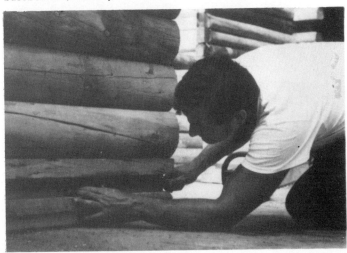

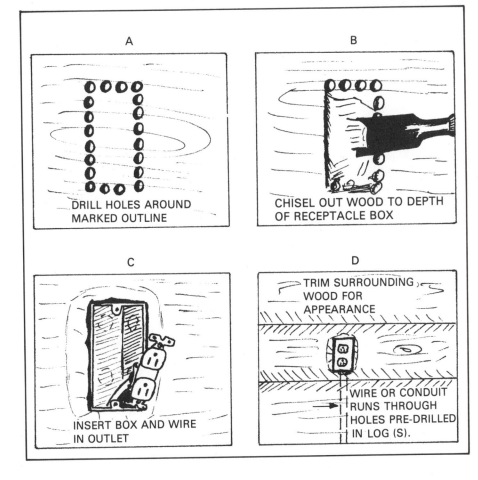

Electrical outlets and switches can be "let in" on log walls. A. mark the outline of the outlet box, then drill close-spaced holes on the lines marked. B. Mortise the notch to necessary depth with a chisel; C. install the box and wire in the switch or outlet; and D. trim the wood around the outlet for appearance. Wires are run through holes that were drilled in the logs before they were laid—measure carefully to make sure holes line up.

123

Run wiring under the floor, between joists, and install most of the outlets and switches in partitions. Some builders install a few outlets in the floor, adjacent to log walls, rather than go to the work of mortising and drilling logs to take outlet boxes.

Or, you can install metallic, multi-outlet surface raceways, with wiring run inside a metal channel capped by a snap-on cover. Outlets, light fixtures and switches can be mounted right in the channel. If you want to change them later, you simply pry off the cover plate to expose the wiring.

For porch lights, doorway lights, doorbells and other fixtures that will be installed at or near exterior doorways, it is fairly simple to build a channel into the door (or window) frame to carry the wiring. Where overhead lighting is to be placed on open joists, beams or girders, a groove can be routed in the top of these members.

For upstairs service in a two-story house, merely run the wiring through a framed partition wall and under the upstairs floor. If the ceiling joists are exposed, you can run the wire along the top of the joist right under the subfloor and conceal it with trim work.

Notches and holes made in floor joists for wires and plumbing should be made so as to least weaken the joists. When running wire through a stud wall, the wire should run through the center of the studs at a uniform height. Keep the location of the wire in mind as you nail on wall covering.

When wiring must run through a wall behind a bathtub or sink, place the wire below the top of these fixtures, to avoid the risk of running a long screw into the wire when you later put up soap dishes, towel bars, etc. Don't run wiring too close to plumbing. Wire insulation can be damaged by the heat from a plumber's torch when sweat connections are made on water lines.

Outlet and switch boxes in partitions should be installed to project the right distance to be flush with the finished wall. For instance, if you will use 3/8-inch gypsum board on the walls, place the boxes so that they extend 3/8 inch past the stud to which they are fastened. Install outlets and switches at a uniform height. A standard height of 12 inches is handy for baseboard receptacles; although you may have to use a different height to make things come out right in log walls. Switches located 48 inches above the floor are at a handy height.

Plumbing

Plumbing consists mainly of getting water from the supply — well, public water main, etc. — to the fixtures in the house, and draining the water and waste it carries

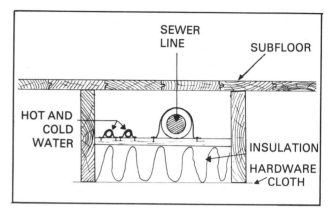

Plumbing run under the floor in a cold basement or crawl space should be protected from freezing.

from the house. Ideally, the water should make this journey and do its work without leaking at any point.

You can use either metal or plastic pipe to run water from the well (or other source) to the house. If you use plastic pipe, install ABS black plastic of at least one inch diameter and designed to withstand pressures up to 125 pounds per square inch.

Whatever kind of water supply piping you use, it should be buried below the frost line or protected from freezing with insulation or electric heat tape. Plastic pipe should be protected against damage by rocks, also. You can do this by putting a layer of sand in the bottom of the water line trench, placing the pipe on this sand and covering it with three to four inches of sand, before the trench is back-filled with the excavated dirt.

The water supply usually is brought into the house through the basement or crawl space. You should install a stop-and-waste valve where the supply pipe joins the house plumbing. This lets you close the valve to shut off the water supply and drain the house plumbing — in case you need to do general repair work, make additions to the plumbing, or protect pipes from freezing if the house will be unheated in cold weather.

Sewer Systems

If you build your house where no public sewer main is available, the best one-dwelling sewer system is probably a septic tank and disposal field. In some areas, cesspools and open lagoons for waste treatment are still permitted, but these are rapidly being outlawed as unsatisfactory and unsafe.

The disposal field should be designed for the soil type, as well as for the number of persons occupying the house. You will need a larger disposal field for tighter, less permeable soils. The table on the facing page is a rough guide of the length of disposal line needed in various soil types:

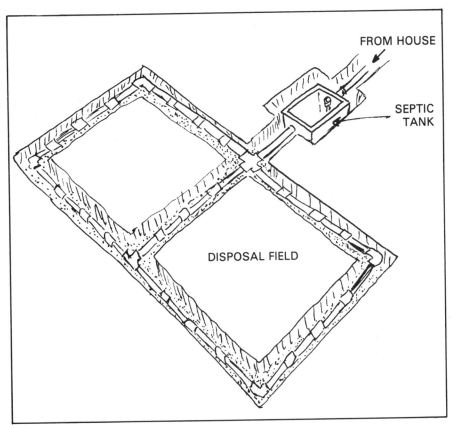

Size of the septic tank will depend on local codes, and the number of persons occupying the house. Length of disposal laterals depends on the soil type.

FROM HOUSE

SEPTIC TANK

DISPOSAL FIELD

Soil type	Ft. of line per bedroom
Gravel	40 feet
Sand	60 feet
Loam	100 feet
Clay	160 feet

Family size (No. of persons)	Tank capacity (gallons)
4 or less	350
4-6	550
6-8	600
8-10	750
10 or more	1,000

With some soil types — those with poor absorption — the disposal field for a septic tank may require that many tons of rock, sand or gravel be hauled in and placed in the disposal "lateral" trenches. Building sites in low or flat areas may require considerable earth-moving to get the required slope to drain lines and septic disposal fields.

Septic tanks can be made of concrete, steel or other material. In most areas, prefabricated tanks are available, built to the proper size and design for good operation.

Local codes may have specific size requirements for septic tanks, or you can use this guide to plan the size of your unit:

Note. Large families, with a lot of laundry to do, may want to run separate drainage lines to a small septic tank for wash water. The volume of water, plus the inhibiting quality of nonbiodegradable detergents on bacteria, can overload a solid-waste disposal tank.

Drain lines from the house to the septic tank, and from the tank to the disposal field, must be sloped at the proper pitch for proper drainage. The guide is that the drain pipe should slope not less than 1/8 inch nor more than 1/2 inch per four feet of pipe. Pipes pitched less than 1/8 inch per four feet do not have enough slope for the water and solid waste to move fast enough to keep the pipe clean. In pipes pitched more than 1/2 inch per

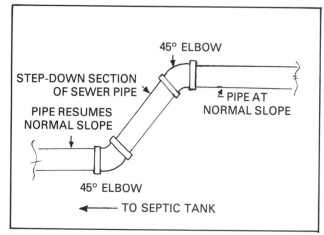

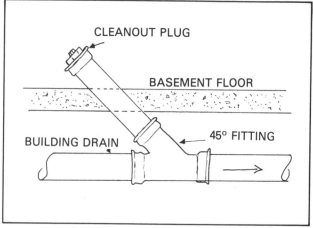

Sewer drainpipes should be pitched at less than one-half inch per foot of run, or 45 degrees or more from the horizontal—one or the other. For steeply sloping building sites, pipe can be "stepped-down" with 45-degree elbows (called 1/8 bends) then continued at a normal pitch.

Drains should have clean-outs installed. One clean-out in the basement or crawl space may be ample for drains with short runs to the septic tank. For longer distances, a second clean-out at mid-point is handy.

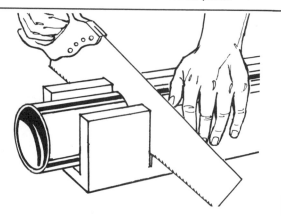

Step 1—Cut pipe to length desired. A mitre box and cross-cut saw will assure square ends for correct sealing in socket type fittings.

Step 2—With cloth, wipe dirt, oil, or water from fitting socket.

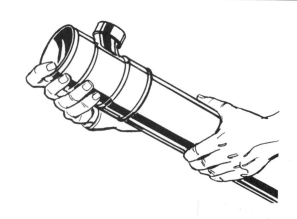

Step 3—Clean pipe end of burrs, dirt, etc. Apply ABS Solvent to pipe end, Brush on ABS Solvent in inside of fitting socket.

Step 4—Join fitting and pipe. Sets in two minutes for a permanent leak proof joint.

Plastic drain piping is easy to work with, and cheaper than metal pipe (Courtesy of Sears, Roebuck and Company)

four feet, the water outruns the solid material which builds up and clogs the pipe eventually.

If drainage pipes must be run with more than 1/2 inch per four foot pitch, as on steeply sloping sites, the pipe should be designed with "step-down" sections of 45-degree drops between the lengths of pipe laid at the proper pitch.

Inside the house, the drainage piping should be planned to limit the cutting of framing members. In log houses, the plumbing will normally run under floors and through partitions; it is impractical to try to run pipes through a solid log wall.

Drainage systems should be vented to the atmosphere above the roof. If the plumbing is fairly well concentrated, as where kitchen and bathroom are placed back-to-back, one three-inch vent stack is sufficient to vent any sewer gas and allow the drain to function properly. Where the plumbing is more scattered, each area should be vented.

Laying Out The System

It is economical, both when building and later, to keep as much of the plumbing as possible concentrated in one area of the house. Kitchen and bathroom or utility room can be planned to occupy opposite sides of a partition wall, to cut down on the amount of material and labor to plumb these rooms. In two-story houses, bathrooms can be "stacked" one over the other, for the same reason.

There's another good reason to congregate the plumbing. Hot water cools off if it has to stand, or travel

long distances between the water heater and the outlet. You can, of course, partly offset this by insulating hot water lines.

Each fixture — sink, dishwasher, lavatory, toilet, tub, etc. — should be equipped with its own shut-off valve. This adds cost when you are buying and installing material, but it comes in handy when repairs must be made . . . and repairs are needed in any home as time goes on.

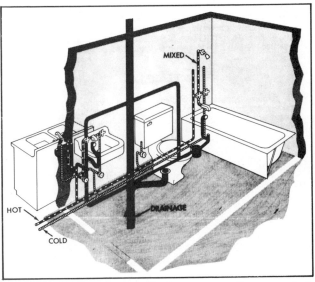

Back-to-back kitchens and bathrooms, or utility rooms, help cut plumbing costs. (Courtesy of USDA Forest Service)

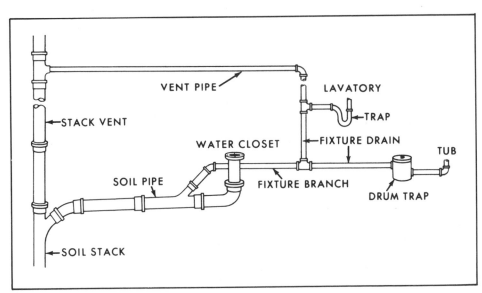

Drains should be vented to the atmosphere. A 3-inch vent stack usually is sufficient to vent one bathroom and kitchen. (Courtesy of USDA)

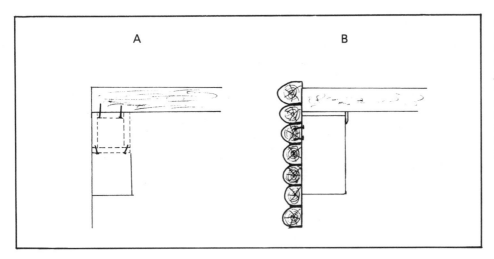

Kitchen wall cabinets can be attached to a "dropped ceiling" soffit, which in turn is nailed to the bottom of ceiling joists, as in figure A. Or, cabinets can be attached to one course of logs, with a space above the cabinets, as shown in figure B. Both methods allow for settling of logs in the wall.

"Eat-in" kitchens can make good use of space in a log home. Designs shown are: A. U-shaped layout; B. L-shaped layout; and C. straight-line layout.

Bathrooms should be planned for the family they will serve. A. minimum bathroom; B. compartmented bathroom; and C. bathroom with shower stall. (Courtesy of USDA)

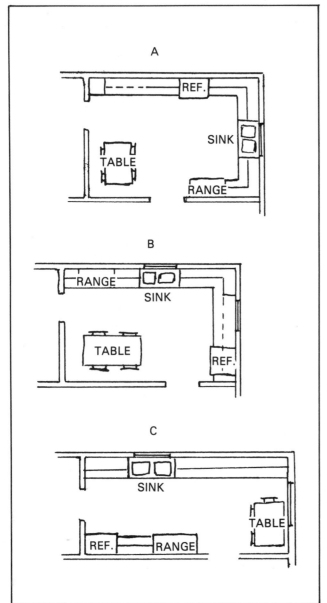

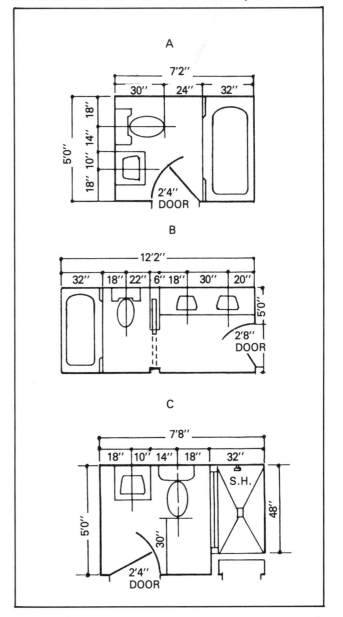

Pipes

For both hot and cold water lines, copper remains the best choice. Be sure you anchor copper pipe with copper brackets or hangers, and use copper nails to attach the brackets, since copper reacts with steel and other metals to produce an electro-galvanic action that deteriorates copper.

Plastic pipe is cheaper to buy and easier to install then copper. However, codes in some areas prohibit the use of plastic, particularly for hot water service. Plastic pipe has been improved to where it is a close second to copper in quality and serviceability, despite some of the bureaucratic sanctions against its use.

The simplest way to run water service to kitchen and bathroom sinks may be to bring water lines up through the floor from the basement or crawl space. The floor connections can be hidden by vanity cabinets in bathrooms and by cabinets in the kitchen. You can also bring the water supply for the toilet through the floor.

The plumbing that serves a bathtub should be run through a wall. This is not difficult since, in most cases, bathtubs are located against a wall anyway. It's a good idea to build an access panel on the other side of the wall, opposite the bathtub plumbing.

When installing plumbing fixtures and other components in kitchens and bathrooms, remember (again) that log walls can settle.

Cabinets

Kitchen cabinets should not be installed right up against ceiling joists, but should have a space above them. For best results, the cabinets should hang from one course of logs. Better yet, build a soffit that is suspended from ceiling joists. This will allow the house wall to settle without affecting the cabinets.

Keep this settling in mind when you place kitchen counters, refrigerators, built-in ranges and ovens, shower stalls and other units. These should not be placed directly under wall cabinets or other components that will prevent logs from moving as they settle and shrink.

Through-floor plumbing may be the simplest method for bathrooms and kitchens located along a log wall. (Courtesy of Sears, Roebuck and Company)

A bathtub full of water weighs several hundred pounds. Be sure the tub is braced firmly.

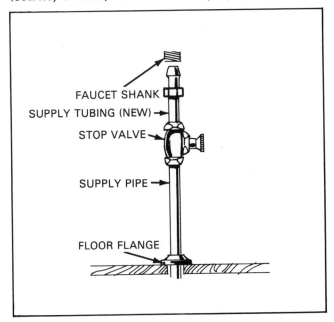

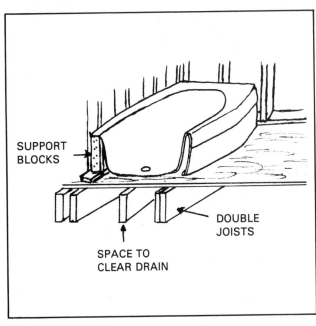

The Heating System

In general, the same kind of heating systems can be used with log homes as with houses of any other construction: hot-water, forced-draft furnace, electric baseboard heaters, wall furnaces, etc. About the only provision that is unique to log construction is that ducts and piping should be planned to utilize under-floor and through-partition locations.

Ducts for forced-draft heat or airconditioning systems usually are installed in the floor at the base of exterior walls. This involves cutting through the subfloor. Short pieces of lumber, of the same dimensions as joist material, can be nailed in as blocking to help support the floor around ducts and grills.

Cold-air returns are located in partition walls, with the studs on either side of the intake forming the duct. The subfloor and sole plate will need to be cut out at the bottom of the wall. The space immediately below, between floor joists, is enclosed with flat sheet metal (called "panning") to serve as the cold-air return under the floor.

Electric baseboard heaters along log walls usually are recessed into notches cut into the bottom log. Another solution is to run a trimmed baseboard around the bottom of the log wall and install the heaters in this member. In this method, the wiring need not be notched into the log but can be run behind the baseboard.

Installing electrical, plumbing, and heating services in a log house will be much easier if the work is planned and laid out before building begins. It is time-consuming — and usually messy — to rip off wall coverings to put electrical wiring or water pipes in the wall once paneling or sheet rock is up. You may have to do a lot of this if you are remodeling or rebuilding an existing log home. But with new construction, whether from a kit or from scratch, provisions for all utilities should be made as the work progresses.

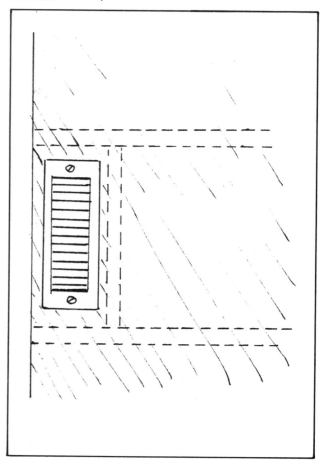

Where flooring must be cut for the installation of heating registers and ducts, brace the subflooring with a piece of lumber the same dimensions as floor joist material.

13.

ENERGY-SAVING HOUSES

Whether you are building a new log home or re-doing an older one, there are several ways you can incorporate features now to save money on future heating and cooling costs. You can also plan your house to save energy in other areas.

Whatever heating system you install, your home should be built to keep heat inside during the winter and to keep outside heat from getting in during the summer. The extra cost involved in building an airtight, well-insulated house will be returned within a few years through savings in fuel and power bills.

Insulate Well

Insulating floors, ceilings and walls probably will save more energy dollars than any other single thing a home builder can do. Costs of insulation materials have climbed during the past few years, but it's still fairly inexpensive and easy to install.

How much insulation to use in a home is largely an economic decision — and perhaps somewhat of an aesthetic consideration with log home owners, if added insulation means covering up the inside log walls. Balance the fuel savings against the initial cost of insulation to arrive at an optimum level of insulation.

Insulation commonly is measured in "R values," a term used to describe the resistance to heat movement through a material. The higher the R value, the greater the resistance to heat flow. "R" is an additive quality: two inches of a given material will have twice the R value of one inch. The individual R values for all materials in a given section of a structure — ceiling, wall, etc. — are added together to obtain the cumulative R value or total insulation. The following table gives the R value per inch of thickness for commonly used insulation and building materials:

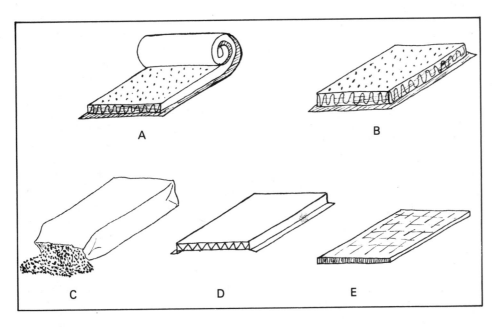

Insulation Types: (A) roll, with vapor barrier; (B) batt, with vapor barrier; (C) loose fill; (D) reflective; and (E) rigid.

Material	R value per inch
Fiberglass; mineral wool (batts)	3.7
Fiberglass; mineral wool (loose)	4.0
Wood fiber	4.0
Vermiculite	2.3
Shredded pulp or paper	4.2
Expanded polystyrene	4.0
Expanded polyurethane foam	6.3
Insulation sheathing board	2.6
Plywood	1.3
Cedar; cypress	1.3

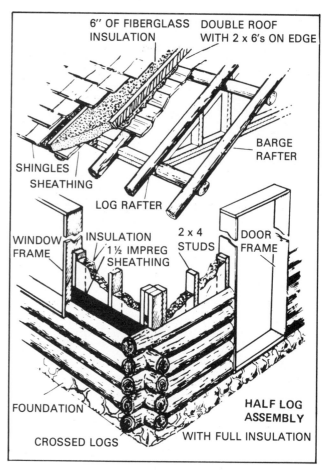

Unique half-log construction in Wilderness Log Homes' precut kits utilize framed inside walls and 3½ inches of insulation. Upper drawing shows construction of insulated "double" roof over open rafters. (Drawings Courtesy Wilderness Log Homes, Inc.)

Log walls often are covered with sheetrock, laminate or tile in kitchens and bathrooms. Furring strips of 1X2 or 2X2, with insulation between, make a plumb gridwork for wall covering materials and increase the R value of walls.

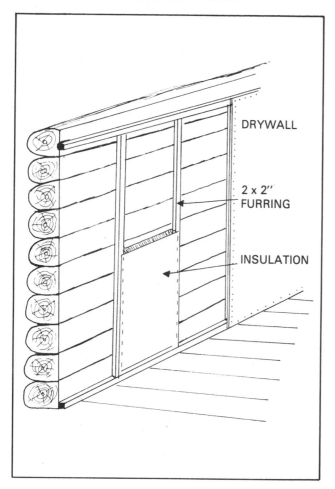

It would take 10 inches of poured concrete to equal the insulating value of one inch of ash wood; and it would take about 7½ inches of ash wood to equal the insulating value of one inch of polyurethane foam.

Let's say your open-beam ceiling is constructed of one-inch tongue-and-groove pine, two inches of polyurethane foam, three-quarters inch of plywood, a layer of 30-pound roofing felt and butt-type asphalt shingles. Add the R values of the various materials to get the cumulative insulation of the ceiling: sheathing, 1.0; urethane foam, 12.6; plywood, 0.97. This provides a total of about 14.5 in R value, plus whatever insulating properties are contained in the roofing felt and shingles.

Take another case: let's say your home is built of six-inch-thick red cedar logs, with the joints insulated and well-caulked to prevent air seepage. With an R value of about 1.3 per inch, the total R value of the walls will be 7.8.

Ceiling insulation of R-14.5 and wall insulation of R-7.8 is about the right ratio. Since heat rises, insulation emphasis should be on the ceiling.

Stopping Heat Leaks

The weathertightness and heating/cooling efficiency of house construction cannot be measured by insulation thickness alone. The house described above may well be warmer in winter and cooler in summer — with less energy consumed — than one with 15 inches of fiberglass (R-38) in the ceilings and 3½ inches of fiberglass (R-11) in the framed sidewalls. Fifteen inches of fiberglass in the ceiling cannot stop air from seeping in around windows, under doors and at other points.

Several areas in a home may be neglected when insulating. Walls separating living areas from attached garage or basements may not have been insulated (it's nearly impossible to keep a garage warm, because of air leaking around and through garage doors). Insulation in the wall between the house and garage will reduce heat flow from the warm house to the cold garage. The same is true of walls and ceilings of unheated basements.

Attic insulation is most important, since heat rises. Loose insulation can be poured and leveled in spaces between joists, as shown.

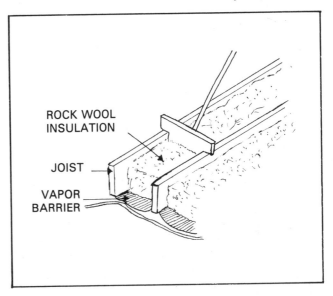

ROCK WOOL INSULATION

JOIST

VAPOR BARRIER

How a heat pump works: During cooling cycle, refrigerant absorbs heat as it passes through the indoor coil (1) and cools air inside the house. Blower (2) pushes cooled air through ducts. Compressor (3) pumps refrigerant through the refrigerant cycle (4) where it releases the heat it has picked up. Outdoor fan (5) pushes heat off into the atmosphere. During the heating cycle, the process is reversed. The refrigerant (1) collects heat from outside air, while the outdoor fan (2) pushes cooled air out. Reversing valve on the compressor (3) causes refrigerant to flow in the opposite direction from cooling cycle, and to release heat as it passes through the indoor coil (4). Indoor fan (5) pushes heated air through ducts in the house, and supplemental heat (6) is activated by a thermostat when cold weather overcomes the rate of heat collection.

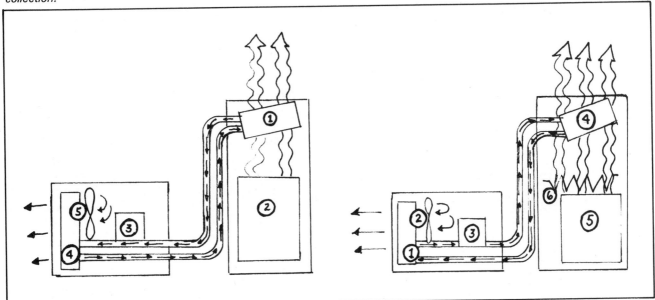

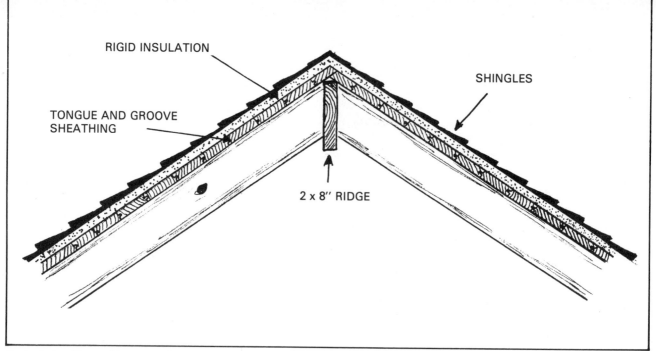

RIGID INSULATION

SHINGLES

TONGUE AND GROOVE SHEATHING

2 x 8" RIDGE

Cathedral ceilings with open rafters or purlins can be insulated with rigid foam sheets fastened to the roof sheathing.

Narrow cracks around window and door framing represent a relatively small amount of total exterior surface; however, these small cracks can leak a lot of air. Heat required to warm the cold outside air that creeps into a house can amount to half of the annual fuel bill.

Another frequent problem is moisture. All air contains moisture, but warm air can hold a lot more of it than cold air. During winter months, the air inside a house is warmer than outside air, and moisture is continually added to it during normal everyday living — washing, cooking, respiration.

Moisture in air behaves pretty much the same way as heat — it moves from areas of high concentration (inside the house) to areas of low concentration (outside). If it meets a cold surface during this migration, moisture condenses out into free water. When this happens inside an insulated wall, the insulation becomes damp and loses much of its insulating value. That's why vapor barriers are installed over the *inside* face of insulated surfaces. The vapor barrier prevents moisture, in the form of water vapor, from getting to cold surfaces where it can condense.

So, on balance, the value of insulation depends heavily on how well a building is constructed. A home wrapped in a lighter blanket of insulation — of whatever source — but with controlled moisture may be more energy efficient than a home with heavier insulation that has been carelessly installed.

Other Heat Holders

Use double-glazed windows, or storm windows, to reduce heat losses by 30 to 50 percent. Large single-pane glass areas in a wall can radiate unbelievable amounts of heat to the outdoors. You may want to consider fewer or smaller windows, perhaps with screens for ventilation in warmer weather.

Use solid-core doors at exterior openings, and protect them with storm doors. Caulk all cracks around door and window trim.

Seal passages and openings between unfinished attics and heated (or air-cooled) spaces. Insulated crawl spaces and basements help cut down on energy consumption, too.

An "air-lock" sort of entryway with double doors can keep much of the cold air out that normally enters a house when doors are opened.

Seldom-used rooms can be insulated and sealed off from the heated part of the house. For example, a guest bedroom that is used only in summer can be closed off during winter. Rooms with plumbing may need special precautions, however, to keep pipes from freezing. Also insulate pipes and ducts to prevent heating and cooling wastes in basements and crawl spaces.

Ventilation

Keeping a house cool in summer contributes as much to living comfort as heat in winter. In some areas of the country, cooling is more energy-demanding than heating.

As far as insulation and weather-tightness are concerned, virtually the same provisions apply to air-conditioning as to heating. The only difference is, you're trying to keep the hot air outside the house, rather than inside.

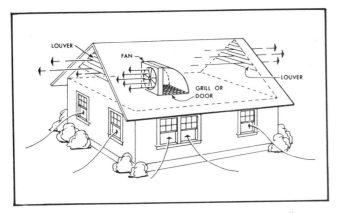

Exhaust fans can be installed in attics, ceilings or walls, to pull hot air from the attic or from living spaces. The drawing above shows one way to install an attic fan. Gable louvers or other vent openings must be large enough to let air escape from the attic. (Drawing courtesy USDA)

Adequate attic ventilation helps prevent solar heat buildup that can radiate to living spaces below. It also helps if you roof the house with light-colored shingles to reflect the sun.

Attic fans, if operated properly, can eliminate the need for air-conditioning in all but the hottest weather. A 30- or 36-inch attic fan can completely change the air in a standard-sized home in a matter of minutes. In the evening, after outside air cools, the windows farthest from the fan can be opened, so the fan can pull cooled air through the house. Then, when the sun gets high next morning, shut off the fan, close the windows and pull drapes to keep the cooled air inside.

Trees on the south and west sides of a house can soak up a lot of the sun's heat, and also shade part of the house. However, avoid having trees so close that limbs damage the roof or prevent log walls from drying quickly after a rain.

More Energy Savers

Space heating and cooling are not the only energy users in an average home. Energy in some form is used to heat water, wash clothes and dishes, cook meals, run appliances and entertainment equipment, provide lighting. There are opportunities for energy — and money — savings in all of these areas.

Many energy-saving features can be planned into a house from the beginning. We've mentioned several in previous chapters; such as concentrating plumbing to save on water heating bills. The water heater should also be located as close as possible to the point of greatest hot water use — usually the kitchen. For example, with a pipe run of 20 feet, you draw nearly two

quarts of cool water before the hot water even reaches the faucet. In a normal household, this amounts to more than 1,000 gallons of water each year — water that is heated but never used. It also means that more water must be pumped, which uses energy.

Another specific approach is in planning house lighting; you may want to use fluorescent fixtures where you can. They use less electricity than incandescent lights of the same candlepower.

If you have central heating, you may want to install a clock-thermostat, with timers to vary temperature settings at different hours of the day.

Little things can make a lot of difference. In the average home, the water heater accounts for 15 percent of the fuel used. Heat controls on water heaters typically are set at about 150 degrees F. (between "medium" and "high" on some control dials). How-

Water heaters typically consume 12 to 15 percent of the total fuel used in the home. Insulating the water heater and hot water lines can reduce the energy used; turning the water temperature down to 120° F. can cut energy usage even more.

ever, if the water temperature is set at 120 degrees, the water still is hot enough for most household uses and the lower setting can trim five to eight percent off the fuel bill. Insulating water heaters and hot water pipes can lead to even more savings.

There are other things you can do to save energy. Some of the following may cost more in time and trouble than the savings is worth in dollars; you'll have to make that judgment yourself:

- dampered vents can be installed on refrigerators and home freezers — in winter, the warmed air from the appliances can be exhausted into the house to help warm the space, while in summer the heated air can be dumped outdoors;
- clothes dryers can be vented to pull their intake air from outdoors in summer, rather than from the cooled house interior — this use of warmer air uses less energy to get the appliance up to drying temperature, too;
- bathroom and kitchen vents can also be designed to exhaust moist, heated air outdoors in summer, and to circulate the air through a chemical filter and back into the house in winter;
- toilets can be adjusted to use less flushing water.

What Kind of Heating System?

As we mentioned in Chapter 12, log homes can be equipped with virtually any kind of heating system. Central heating plants, such as natural gas, LP-gas or fuel oil forced-draft furnaces; heat pumps; electric heat; hot-water heat; or combinations of more than one system are used.

However, there is little question that Americans will have to alter their styles of life in the future, in order to conserve fossil fuels and the electricity they generate. It is even more readily apparent that the cost of conventional sources of energy will continue to climb — rapidly.

Therefore, as you plan the heating system for your log home, keep in mind that petroleum and coal based forms of energy are limited and nonrenewable. That final billion barrels of oil are a nearer reality now than at any time since man began pumping and burning the stuff.

It may be impractical to produce *all* of your own power, at least at the present state of the art, but the more nearly self-sufficient you become the less dependent you are on sources of energy that are vulnerable to

Wood furnaces and combination-fuel burners let home owners enjoy both convenience and economy. This wood furnace is equipped with an LP-gas auxiliary burner that takes over when there is no wood in the firebox. The unit is thermostatically controlled; heated air is ducted throughout a three-bedroom house.

Heat reclaimers installed between a wood-burning stove or furnace and the flue can recover much of the heat that would otherwise escape to the atmosphere. The type of heat reclaimer shown has a small electric blower and can be ducted to one or more rooms.

Arab boycotts, government regulation and other events beyond your property line.

Alternate Systems

As one big oil company's TV commercials put it, there's no real energy shortage — only a *knowledge* shortage. The solar energy falling on just the United States in a year's time could supply perhaps 500 times the energy we now consume, if we only had the knowledge to put it to use.

The same spirit that spurs a man to build his own log house often makes him want to provide for himself in other ways, too. Solar heating, wind-powered electricity generators, methane gas generators, ram water pumps, wood-burning stoves and furnaces of all kinds — these and other alternative energy systems are being developed by individuals as well as commercial firms. Some of the devices built work well; some not so well.

But the point is: anyone with imagination and technical skill has a whole territory in which to "tinker." The months and years ahead will no doubt see sources of energy made practical that aren't even thought of today.

In the short run, perhaps the most workable solution for most families is to combine one or more "home-made" energy systems; or to combine alternate systems with conventional systems. A solar heat collector can be installed to supplement a heat pump or forced-draft gas furnace.

In this vein, several companies now manufacture "dual-fuel" furnaces that burn both wood and LP-gas or fuel oil. Many of these units operate with thermostat controls and blowers to push heated air through ducts to spaces to be heated. When the firebox is kept filled with wood (some of them take logs up to five feet long), this fuel provides the major part of the heat. When the wood burns down, or when no one is at home to refill the firebox, the auxiliary burner takes over and functions much as any other forced-draft furnace.

The most usable form of so-called alternate heating for most log home builders is wood — for space heating, cooking or water heating. Since a big percentage of log home builders choose timbered sites, the wood is available — for the time and cost of cutting it. (There are those who declare that heat from a wood-burning stove or fireplace is somehow superior to heat from other sources, but those claims are difficult to verify objectively.)

The value of wood as fuel varies with species and moisture content. Generally, hardwoods make better fuel than softwoods (conifers), and produce less creosote and gum to collect in stovepipes and flues. The below table gives the approximate Btu's (British Thermal Units) per cord of air-dried wood:

Species	Weight— air-dried	Available heat (Btu's)
Ash	3,400 lbs.	20,000,000
Aspen	2,200 lbs.	12,500,000
Beech	3,760 lbs.	21,800,000
Birch	3,700 lbs.	21,300,000
Douglas Fir	2,400 lbs.	18,000,000
Hickory	4,250 lbs.	24,600,000
Maple	3,200 lbs.	18,600,000
Oak, red	3,700 lbs.	21,300,000
Oak, white	3,900 lbs.	22,700,000
Pine, Eastern white	2,080 lbs.	13,300,000
Pine, Southern	2,600 lbs.	20,500,000

Of course, the usable heat energy in wood may differ from the available heat energy, depending upon how efficient the heating system in which it is burned. You can compare the available heat and relative cost of wood with other fuels. For example, a gallon of home heating oil contains about 140,000 Btu's of heat energy. A cord of air-dried white oak firewood contains 22.7 million available Btu's. That's the equivalent of about 168 gallons of fuel oil. If the wood is burned as an alternate to fuel oil, with the same percentage of efficiency, it's worth $67 per cord, compared with fuel oil at 40 cents per gallon.

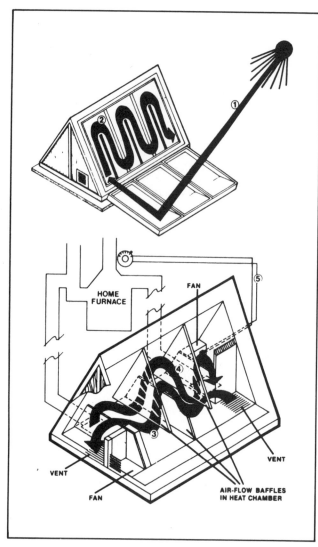

Add-on type solar "furnaces" are compatible with either new construction or existing homes. Solar heat energy is collected at points (1) and (2) in figure A. The heated air is transferred to crushed rock storage, at (3), in figure B. As the thermostat calls for heat, a blower fan (4) circulates air through the rock and into conventional duct work to heat the house. During cloudy periods, the thermostat automatically shifts to the conventional home heating system when heat in the rock storage is used up. (Courtesy International Solarsystems Corp.)

Recent developments in solar space- and water-heating have spurred interest in using the sun's energy directly. However, building a completely solar-heated house is a major undertaking, and the cost probably would be about like building *two* houses.

Still, any home can make some use of the heat radiated on it from the sun. The easiest and simplest method of solar heating is to place most of the windows on the south and let the sun shine through them to heat up the interior of the house. Unfortunately, in most house designs, the windows — unless they are covered at night with some insulative material — probably lose more heat than they collect, for a net heat loss. Also, there's the problem of sun-faded rugs, bedcovers and upholstered furniture.

In most sections of the country, the biggest drawback to solar heating is the fact that the sun doesn't shine every day. That means some system must be devised to collect and store heat — tons of rock or gallons of water — for use at night and on cloudy days.

Another problem, especially with making solar heating as convenient as more conventional systems, is the complicated thermostatic controls required. We have the technology, but there's a price tag on it. Much the same is true of wind-powered electricity generators, methane gas digesters and other alternative energy systems.

The above paragraphs are not at all meant to dissuade those home builders who want to try one or a combination of alternate systems. You may be able to build in an inexpensive solar-heating system that provides 25 to 30 percent of your home heating needs; a wood stove, furnace or fireplace that provides another 60 percent or so; and install space heaters to take up the slack on really cold days.

14.

SHORTCUTS THAT WORK

This chapter is a collection of nice-to-know leftovers that didn't find their way into any of the other sections.

When there are two ways of doing something, both equally productive of a finished result, why not choose the method that takes less time or labor? We've included a number of such methods in this chapter; here are shortcuts that detract in no way from the quality of the finished construction, but speed up the work and make it easier . . . or less expensive.

Foundation and Concrete Work

If you are using concrete blocks for your foundation or basement, here's a fast, accurate way to estimate how many standard (8x8x16 inches) blocks you will need. Multiply the height of each wall by its length, then multiply the result by 1.2. The answer is the approximate number of blocks needed. For example, to find out how many blocks you will need for a wall eight feet tall and 20 feet long, multiply 20 times eight, which gives a product of 160. Multiply 160 times 1.2, to find out that you'll need about 192 blocks.

If you have a supply of long conventional 1/2 or 5/8 inch bolts, you can use them as anchor bolts, rather than buy custom-made "L" bolts to fasten the sill to the

foundation wall. The drawing here shows how to bend the bolts about three inches from the ends, to keep them from turning in the concrete.

Wood or plywood used to build forms for poured concrete often can be used later in other construction, if it is disassembled carefully. To prevent concrete from sticking to wood, coat the wood with a light oil — about 10-weight motor oil. Then, after the concrete is set, the forms can be carefully dismantled and the wood used in places where it will be hidden by other construction.

Floors and Log Walls

The ends of several subflooring boards can be butted against a joist, then cut against another joist. This way, the cut boards will fit center-to-center on the joists. You can use this method to cut roof sheathing, too.

To quickly and accurately measure and mark bridging (the diagonal bracing that is placed between floor joists), lay a piece of floor joist timber squarely across two floor joists and mark both joists at where

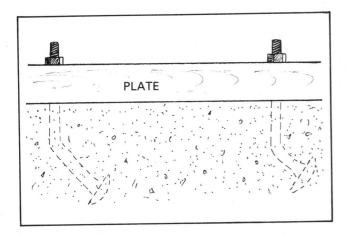

PLATE

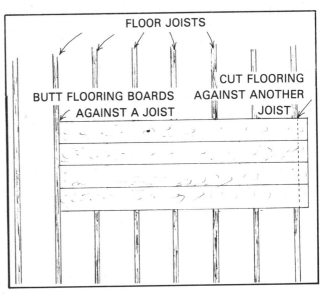

FLOOR JOISTS

BUTT FLOORING BOARDS AGAINST A JOIST

CUT FLOORING AGAINST ANOTHER JOIST

timber crosses them. Now, lay the bridging stock across the joists to line up with the marks. Mark the bridging stock and you have the right cut for fitting the diagonal braces between joists.

Counter-sinking spikes in wall logs is easier if you use a spike-setter. A carriage bolt and nut of the right size to fit over the head of the spike will serve as shown. You can use this same idea to drive nails in inaccessible spots.

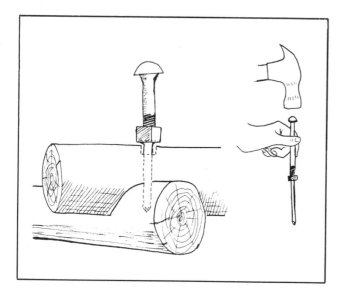

Speaking of nails, the "d" in nail sizes means penny; it used to refer to the cost in pennies for 100 nails. The below table lists the sizes and weights of common nails:

Size	Length	Head Diameter	Number of Nails Per Pound
2d	1 "	11/64"	845
4d	1½"	1/4"	290
6d	2 "	17/64"	165
8d	2½"	9/32"	100
10d	3 "	5/16"	65
12d	3¼"	5/16"	60
16d	3½"	11/32"	45
20d	4 "	13/32"	30
30d	4½"	7/16"	20
40d	5 "	15/32"	17
50d	5½"	1/2"	13
60d	6 "	17/32"	10

You probably will not carry this table with you, so here's an easy way to figure the length of smaller nails (up to 10d). Divide the "penny" size of a nail by four and add ½ inch to get its length in inches. For example, an 8d nail is 2½ inches long (8 divided by 4 equals 2, plus ½ = 2½ inches).

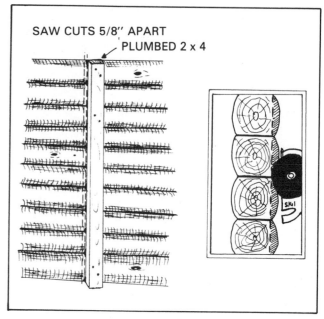

SAW CUTS 5/8" APART
PLUMBED 2 x 4

The accompanying drawing shows a relatively quick and satisfactory way to fit interior framed walls to log walls. Cut two saw grooves up the log wall just the same thickness as the drywall material you will use. Chisel out the wood from between the saw cuts. The paneling or other drywall sheet will slide right into this notch. You don't need to cut a groove for the stud. Just fasten it flush against the log wall, as shown, with a lag screw, in a slot in the stud to allow for settling of the logs.

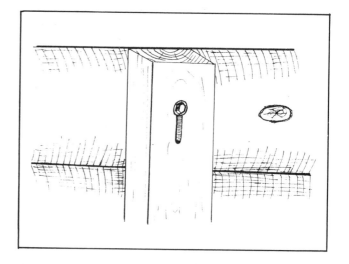

When framing out corners in partitions, make an outside corner with three 2X4 studs, rather than with the four studs normally used. This corner provides a nailing surface for wall covering material and is sufficiently strong for most partitions.

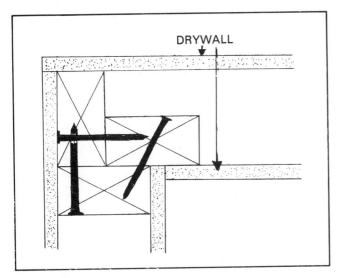

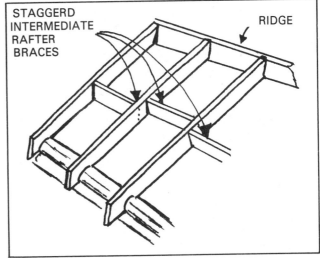

Work on Top

If you are building with rafters that will be open at the eaves (rather than building a closed cornice), you'll need to install snow blocks between the rafters. When rafters are made of dimensional lumber, the blocks are fairly easy to cut and place in order to close gap between the rafters and between the plate and roof sheathing.

You can help prevent leaks at the roof edge from melting ice and snow by extending the roofing felt onto the fascia behind the rain gutter. An even better way is to extend metal flashing from the roof drip edge back under two or three rows of shingles.

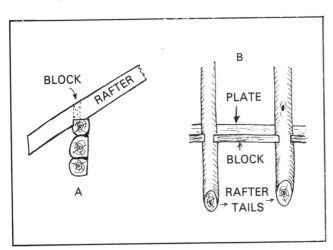

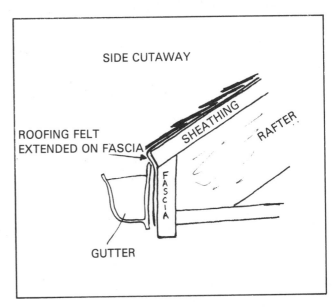

But where pole rafters are used, much cutting and fitting is required to get a tight fit — unless you do it as shown. When you cut the bird's mouth notch, merely continue the back cut of the notch to make a plumb cut on the rafter sides, so that the snow block fits snugly. Notch out as shown in B.

Another time saver is staggered intermediate rafter braces (if you are using them). This allows faster nailing than placement of the braces all in line, and gives ample support to the rafters.

Going Inside

Those 4X8-foot sheets of paneling and other drywall material are cumbersome to cut on a pair of regular saw horses. If you can lay hands on an old kitchen table, it makes a dandy saw table. Remove the center leaf from the table and set the saw's blade depth to just clear the paneling.

There are several rainy-day chores that can help you save time later. Shown is how to nail outlet and switch boxes to wooden blocks cut from scrap lumber. These will be ready to secure to studs or joists when you get to that stage.

Another dose of preventive medicine: long horizontal runs of stove pipe or venting pipe from a furnace or water heater can sag dangerously. In the first place, these pipes should not be run perfectly horizontal, but should have a slight upward pitch toward the flue. You can reinforce such pipes with an angle iron "stiffener" secured to the pipe with sheet metal screws, as illustrated.

You will develop your own building shorthand as you go along — all builders do. Just be sure that any tricks or shortcuts you employ will result in as strong a finished construction as the more conventional ways of building.

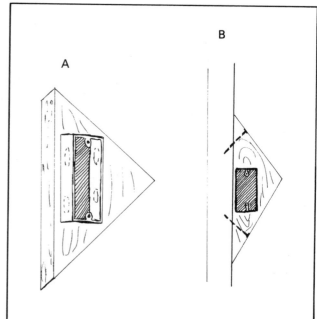

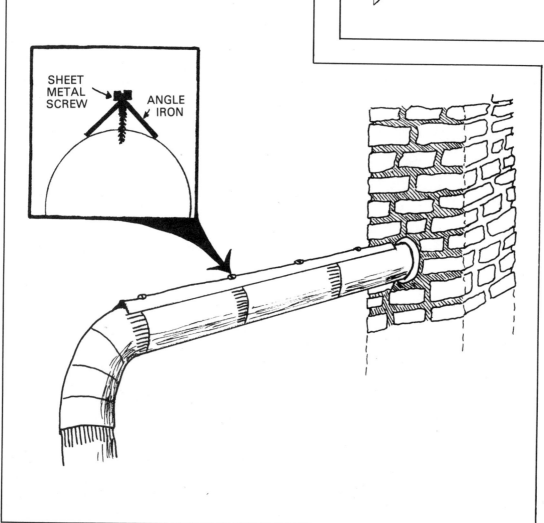

SHEET METAL SCREW

ANGLE IRON

15.

FINISHING &
FURNISHINGS

In general, log homes are best suited to sturdy interior appointments. But even rustic styles can be combined with relaxing atmosphere and ease of maintenance, with a little planning and some carefully chosen finishing materials and furnishings.

The guiding key is: Keep it simple and easy to care for. The building products of modern chemistry — plastics, nylons and other manmade materials — can be used to preserve the character of a log home and cut down on housekeeping chores. Log houses, even those built for full-time residences, usually get more casual treatment and use than other homes. Families who choose to live in log homes typically are more active and carefree than those who prefer ultra-modern dwellings. Because of this, the interior should reflect thoughtful, economic planning for both appearance and easy care.

Walls

Most log home owners like to keep the log walls uncovered — at least in much of the house. Log walls, open beams or rafters provide much of the charm of a log home interior. Some frequent exceptions are kitchens and bathrooms, where logs are furred out with 1X2 or 2X2 strips to which sheetrock, laminate or tile is applied.

Don't be in too big a hurry to stain your log home interior a dark color. Logs darken as they age, and you may want to live with them awhile before you stain them. You can always darken the logs later, but trying to lighten logs that have been stained is an uphill proposition. You can seal logs with one of several products, such as polyurethane sealant, to help preserve the "new" look and make surfaces easier to clean.

By the same token, do not immediately install a great deal of wood paneling on partition walls. The natural logs will usually give enough "wood look" to interiors. Try contrasting them with lighter-hued paints and wallpapers. You can always add paneling later, if you decide that's what you want.

When choosing wallcoverings, don't go to something so flashy that it detracts from the log walls. Logs are a main focal point in log homes — use them that way.

Floors

The key to a good floor lies in understanding the possibilities and limitations of the covering you use, and how well you take care of it.

Wood floors are particularly appropriate to log home designs, but they involve more trouble to install and maintain than some other floor coverings. You can use either softwoods — such as fir or pine — or more durable hardwoods. Wood floors, well finished and coated, can be set off with braided or woven rugs to go well with rustic or Early American furniture styles.

Some log home purists may not agree with their appropriateness, but vinyls, linoleums and other easy-care floor coverings are especially servicable in kitchens, bathrooms, utility rooms and other areas with heavy traffic and occasionally-spilled liquids. These floor coverings come in a variety of patterns and styles; many of which show up well in the company of wood.

Curtains and Carpets

In houses with conventional walls, the objects in a room generally command attention over the walls, ceilings, floors and other "backgrounds." However, the texture and pattern of a log wall may dictate your choices for window curtains and floor coverings.

Light-colored, frilly curtains can help accent bedroom walls and windows. In living rooms and dining rooms, prints and bolder colors can be used for more contrast. Trying to get too fancy doesn't always work, however. Brocades and satins look out of place on a log wall, as do draperies with huge valances and tassels.

Varied textures and patterns complement the natural-log walls. (Courtesy Vermont Log Buildings, Inc.)

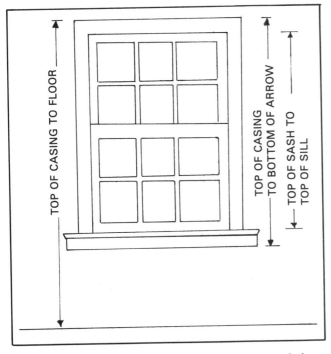

Before buying or making curtains, measure windows for a good fit. For full-length draperies, measure from the top of the window casing to the floor, then subtract one inch for clearance. For cafe curtains, measure either from top of casing to bottom of apron, or top of sash to window sill, depending on style of curtain.

Many log home builders install lightweight wooden shutters, rather than curtains, on windows. This carries the wood theme throughout, and well-designed shutters are even better than curtains for blocking out the sun or holding in heat.

As mentioned earlier, braided or woven area rugs placed over wood floors suit the furnishings many log home dwellers use. However, there is nothing wrong with carpeting in bedrooms, or dining rooms and living rooms. Installed carpeting is more comfortable, quieter and easier to care for than wood floors. Short-shag, multi-colored tweeds show dirt and wear less than longer nap carpets. The predominant colors in the carpet should be on the "warm" end of the spectrum — reds, yellows, beiges — to harmonize with the wood of log walls.

Furnishings — Style vs. Design

Your furnishings should reflect the function of your house and your family's style of living. What is good for one individual or household is not necessarily right for another, of course. A good starting point, when you are considering the furnishings that suit your log home, is to distinguish between style and design.

Esther Hales long had wished for a log home to house both her family and her collection of family heirlooms and antiques. This photo and the one on the following page show many of the items that can be displayed in the living room, dining room, and kitchen.

Style is more faddish — a mode of the times. It is influenced by many things and changes from year-to-year or decade-to-decade. Period furniture at times bears the name of a monarch or dynasty whose taste dictated the style.

Design is more closely related to function. While style changes, good design endures. A chair or couch may be stylish, but if it is uncomfortable to sit on, it is not well designed.

For log home interiors, furniture that is designed more nearly for pure function usually is more suitable than furnishings with a lot of decorative detail. A dainty French Provincial chair alongside a wall of massive, solid-wood logs would look sorely out of place. So would furniture that features a lot of metal, chrome, marble or plastic.

Stick to the Basics

The furniture you choose, and spend money for, should satisfy your own taste and fill the functional needs of your home. It will be on close terms with you and other members of your family for years. Choose well.

Log homes, as mentioned above, are rarely the place for cute and clever decorations and furnishings.

Fancy and ultra-formal appear out of place in the more rustic, "country" atmosphere of log construction. Broad lines, thick forms and unbroken surfaces pick up the "feel" of a log wall and contribute to a sense of mass and weightiness in a room. Chairs, tables, chests of drawers and other common pieces should be strong, meet the needs of the owner and relate well to other objects in the room.

One basic of interior design is to determine the focal point, or points, of a room, then plan the placement of furniture and accessories to emphasize this center of interest. The focal point may be a fireplace, the center of a long wall, a picture grouping or other visual center of interest.

As noted above, the logs themselves can provide a focal point. This can either simplify or complicate your choice and placement of furniture and other decorations in a room. It may mean that you will have to "create" a dominant focal point in some rooms; a center of interest around which everything else is subordinated.

You may want to study each room before any furniture or decorations are placed in it. Walk into the room, as if you were entering it for the first time ever. Be aware of the overall appearance, space, size and entire mood of the room.

Is the room relatively long and narrow, or more nearly square in shape? Are there long, unbroken wall lines? Or do doors, windows and other openings chop up the wall space into shorter pieces? Does the room

Brass Woodbasket

Brass Coal Hod

Fireplace bellows. Brass, Naugahyde and walnut.

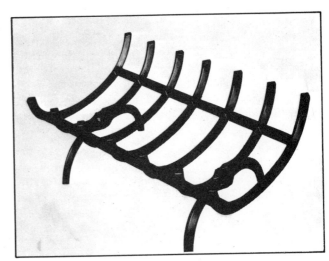

Log grate with open ends works well with a log-home fireplace.

The Hales family puts their antique collection to use on the front porch, as well as in the house. An old neck-yoke and kerosene lantern lights the porch. (Notice the small bell at the end of the yoke.) Old church pews bracket the front door.

have a low smooth ceiling, or a high cathedral-type ceiling with open tie beams and rafters or purlins?

As you study the room, try to visualize how the space would look with different placements of furniture and accessories. A partition wall opposite a log wall may be the best place to hang pictures or mirrors. A long room may be arranged into more than one subdivision — perhaps one end with the fireplace as a focal point; the other end arranged to center on another interesting feature. Floor coverings and wall coverings can help emphasize the different areas, also.

It often helps to make a scale outline drawing of the room, with focal points sketched in. Cutouts to represent furniture pieces can be moved about on the layout—much easier than furniture can be moved about a room.

Going Americana

By far the most popular look in log home decorating is that broad, general category best described as "Americana." These highly personal mixes of family heirlooms, collected antiques, copper pots, Early American and contemporary furnishings and accessories seem particularly at home in log houses.

There are no hard and fast rules, other than avoiding obvious clutter and jarring contrasts. You can mix and match whatever combinations you choose to surround yourself with. Wood plays a big role in Americana, and does wrought iron, brass, wicker, leather and coarser fabrics.

Greenery, house plants potted in everything from antique milk cans to nail kegs, goes well in Americana-decorated log homes. Macrame work of jute or hemp sets off wood and hand-painted ceramics in hanging plants from open beams and ceiling joists.

In short, "do your own thing," as the saying goes. Professional designers might cringe at some contrasts and combinations, but professional designers themselves often disagree on what is proper and harmonious. Use whatever suits your home, your style of living and your budget.

148

16.

PRESERVATION & MAINTENANCE

Once construction is completed, a well-built log home is fairly easy to maintain.

Moisture Problems

The best protection against decay for any house is to keep it dry—inside and out. Decay organisms cannot survive at moisture levels below 30 percent. Air-dried wood located more than 10 inches above the ground surface typically is well below that moisture content.

Here are some things to watch for when building and after the house has been completed

Foundations

The basement or foundation wall may remain damp for some time after a house has been built. Concrete requires several weeks to cure completely. If the house has been built properly on a well-drained site, the dampness should be driven out by the first winter's heating of the house interior.

Frequent inspections of the area where wooden members join masonry walls will spot potential trouble that can develop after construction; such as leaking gutters or downspouts, soil that has settled at the foundation and formed water-holding pockets, signs of moisture and decay in wood members, etc.

Under houses with crawl spaces, the soil supplies water vapor to the air. In winter, this moisture can condense on cold sills and joists and can wet the wood to the point where decay fungi can attack it. Cross-ventilation under the house helps prevent this moisture buildup. Better still, a vapor barrier of plastic, building felt or other moisture-proof material will stop the moisture at its source.

You'll also want to watch for termite activity in areas where these wood-eaters are potential problems. Termite shields installed below the bottom framing members and an insecticide treatment of the soil in crawl spaces and around foundations help ward off termites. But check also for the tell-tale mud tubes on concrete walls or piers. Termites can enter a building through cracks in the foundation wall.

Any openings that develop between the basement wall and the sill plate (or sill log) should be filled with cement mortar or caulking compound.

Caring for Walls

The ideal situation is to use naturally decay-resistant logs, or logs that have been pressure-treated with a preservative. However, not all log home builders have these materials available. The next best alternative is to apply a preservative to the logs after they are in place—and regularly thereafter.

Preservatives. The exterior walls need no painting (heaven forbid!) or staining, but should be sprayed with a preservative. These treatments may be as frequent as once each year for homes built in humid southern states, or only once every three to four years for houses in colder, dryer climes.

Spraying is much more effective than brushing or swabbing the preservative. Use enough preservative to thoroughly wet the wood from top to bottom. Give extra heavy applications to corners, joints and the lower courses of logs nearer the ground. Figure on using 20 gallons or more of the diluted preservative for an average-sized home for each treatment. A fruit-tree hand sprayer is a useful apparatus for applying preservatives.

What kind of preservative you use depends on what's available and recommended for your area — and comparative costs. Pentachlorophenol at five percent concentration in fuel oil or other carrying agent is used most often. Several commercial preservatives use penta as the active agent.

Copper naphthenate, at two percent copper concentration also is effective. Both penta and copper napthenate are relatively odorless and do not stain logs.

Coal-tar creosote also can be used, but creosote stains logs a dark color and smells to high heaven. Since most preservative treatments are made in warm weather, when windows are open, the odor of creosote can linger inside the house for some time.

Of course, windows and doors should be closed while the preservative is being applied. Ideally, they should be covered with plastic bags, old window shades or some other material; most preservatives leave a sticky residue that is hard to remove from glass.

Pick a quiet, windless day to do your spraying. Wear gloves, goggles, long-sleeved shirt and long trousers. You may want to tie the cuffs of pants' legs and wear a respirator, as well. Make the entire area off-limits to kids and pets. Keep in mind that all wood preservatives are poisonous. They have to be to destroy insects and decay fungi. These materials can burn the skin and eyes painfully, so use and store them with caution.

Most log home owners do nothing to inside walls. However, you can brighten up logs and put a smooth finish on them — for easier cleaning and to preserve that new look — with boiled linseed oil or polyurethane sealer.

Windows and Doors

If the wooden parts of doors and windows and their frames are to be left "natural" or varnished, they should be coated with linseed oil. Apply the linseed oil to the glazing as well, to prevent cracking and the premature need for reglazing. Vinyl- or plastic-clad windows need no other treatment.

Joints between logs, cracks in logs and around window and door frames should be tightly caulked to prevent moisture from entering the wood. Moisture, and the decay it encourages, is a major cause of rot damage in all kinds of houses.

Roof gutters and downspouts are good preservation equipment. Gutters should be sloped slightly from a high point to the downspout. Lower ends of downspouts should discharge water three feet or more from the house foundation, using either a splash block or plastic hose.

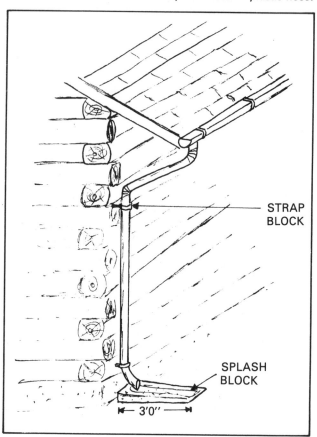

STRAP BLOCK

SPLASH BLOCK

3'0"

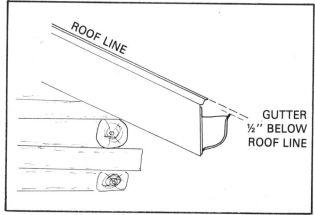

ROOF LINE

GUTTER ½" BELOW ROOF LINE

Gutters should be installed so that the outer edge of the gutter is slightly below the roof line. This helps prevent "ice dams", which impound water that can seep under shingles.

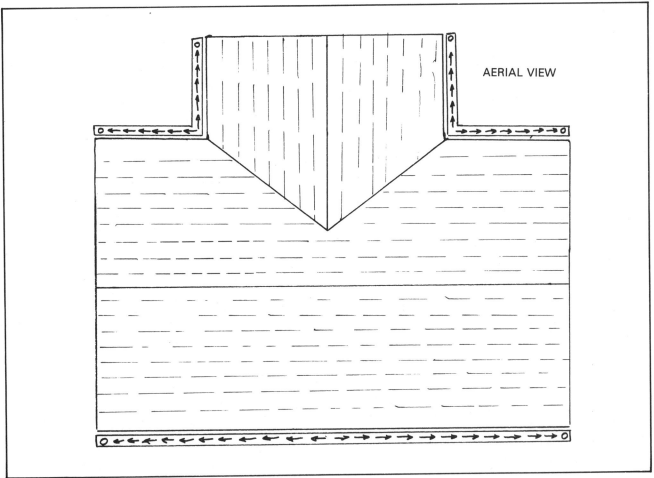

AERIAL VIEW

The rain gutter should not exceed 20 feet in length. For roof lines greater than 20 feet, make the highest point of the gutter in the center of the roof and slope towards each end.

Even with treatments, window sashes may discolor with time, especially in colder climates where water condenses on the inside of the glass and runs down to seep into the wood. Storm sashes or double-pane windows help prevent this condensation.

Flashing above horizontal surfaces and projections, such as door and window casings, protect windows from rain water seepage. Use corrosion-resistant metal for the flashing.

Exterior doors should also be coated with polyurethane sealer or linseed oil. This should be done soon after the door is installed, to prevent the wood from swelling and shrinking with moisture changes. Apply a coating of the sealant to wooden door treads at the same time.

The condition of caulking around doors, windows and other openings should be checked as you inspect the exterior of your house.

Roofs and Gutters

Roofs with wide overhangs, both at the eaves and gable ends, provide a lot of protection to the rest of the house exterior, by shading it from the sun and shielding it from the rain.

In areas with heavy snowfalls, metal flashing should extend from the roof edge back under the lower courses of shingles, to keep melting snow from backing up behind shingles and leaking down into the cornice or walls.

Check the flashing at valleys, ridges, around the chimney and where plumbing vent stacks go through the roof. Look for loose shingles, loosened metal flashing and dried out and cracked asphalt cement.

Gutters and downspouts are helpful in carrying the roofshed water away from the house and foundation. These must be inspected and maintained regularly. Clean clogged gutters and downspouts, and look for loosened joints in the guttering. At the lower end of the downspout, the water should be directed away from the house by a hose, splash block or storm sewer connection.

Fireplaces and Chimneys

Inspect chimneys and flues each summer after wood-burning season is over.

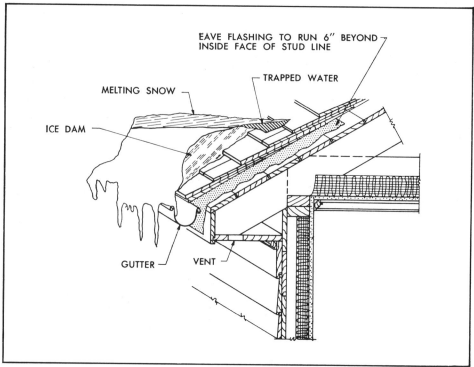

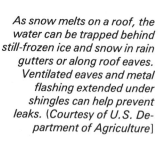

As snow melts on a roof, the water can be trapped behind still-frozen ice and snow in rain gutters or along roof eaves. Ventilated eaves and metal flashing extended under shingles can help prevent leaks. (Courtesy of U.S. Department of Agriculture]

EAVE FLASHING TO RUN 6" BEYOND INSIDE FACE OF STUD LINE

TRAPPED WATER

MELTING SNOW

ICE DAM

GUTTER   VENT

If green or wet wood is burned in cold weather, creosote may form in the flue. Usually, the greatest deposits of creosote will be above the point where the chimney comes through the roof, where flue gases cool and allow the creosote and tars to condense out.

These deposits create a fire hazard, and are often difficult to remove. About the only way is to mechanically chip the stuff from the flue liner.

Commercial soot removers, which are thrown into the stove or fireplace while a fire is burning, can help keep soot and creosote deposits from collecting in flues. Common rock salt is about as effective, and much cheaper to use. If you plan to use some kind of chemical soot remover, start using it with a clean flue. These materials cause the soot to burn, in flues with heavy accumulations of soot and creosote, and may result in a chimney fire.

Porches and Stoops

Porch steps, floors, posts and railings are exposed to the weather and therefore more susceptible to decay than those parts of the house that are better protected.

Porches can be designed to shed water, as mentioned in Chapter 10, to help ward off decay and moisture damage. Slope porch floors to allow water to drain off. Provide good ventilation under the floor. Set stairs and steps on concrete well above the ground surface.

Wood preservative should be applied to porch posts and other framing members that are closest to the soil. A thick coating of asphalt cement or white lead on the lower end of porch posts and pillars also helps prevent moisture seepage into these members.

In summary, if you have built a well-designed house of seasoned, air-dried wood and keep it dry, you can ward off decay almost indefinitely with just a little maintenance. It's hard to over-emphasize the importance of regular inspections of those potential trouble spots listed in this chapter.

If you spot a developing problem early, prevention is usually easy—and cheap. Cures of problems long neglected are invariably expensive.

APPENDIX

GLOSSARY OF BUILDING TERMS

Air-dried (*logs*)   Wood that has been stacked for seasoning for length of time. Completely air-dried wood contains 15 to 20 percent moisture.

Anchor bolts   Steel bolts used to fasten wooden framing members to concrete or masonry walls.

Backfill   The replacement of excavated earth against a foundation or basement wall.

Batter boards   Horizontal boards nailed to posts at the corners of a building outline to mark the desired level, as of a foundation wall.

Beam   A horizontal structural member supporting a load; i.e. the member that supports floor joists in the center of a house.

Bearing partition   An interior wall that supports a vertical load.

Bevel cut   An angled cut in a piece of material that is something other than square or perpendicular to the stock being cut.

Bird's mouth cut   A notch cut into the lower end of a rafter that will extend beyond a wall. The cut is a 90-degree angle notch that allows the rafter to lie flush on the top of the wall or plate.

Blue stain   A blue or gray discoloration of sapwood, caused by infection with a fungus.

Board foot   Designates 144 cubic inches of lumber.

Brace   An angled piece of framing used to strengthen a wall, floor or rafter.

Bridging   Wooden or metal diagonal braces installed between floor joints at mid-span.

Butt joint   A joint of two pieces of material where structural strength is not a factor. The two members are cut square and joined at the square-cut surfaces.

Casing   Moldings used to trim door and window openings at jambs.

Caulking   Material used to close seams or joints between logs or other members, to provide an airtight, watertight seal.

Checking   Cracks and fissures that appear in wood with age and drying.

Chinking   Material used to fill larger cracks and spaces between logs; usually of oakum, mortar or other material bonded to lath of wire mesh or hardware cloth.

Collar tie (or collar beam)   The horizontal timber that ties two opposite walls or pairs of rafters, to prevent the spreading apart of walls under weight.

Cornice   The overhang of a roof at the eave; the fascia, soffit and moldings that enclose the eave.

Crawl space   A space beneath the first floor of a basementless house, usually enclosed by a foundation.

Drawknife   A sharp steel blade with handles on both ends, at right angles to the blade, used for trimming wood.

Drip cap   Flashing or molding placed over the top of an exterior door or window frame to divert water from the frame.

Drywall   Any interior wall covering that is applied without masonry; such as paneling or sheetrock.

Eave   The lower part of a roof projection.

Fascia   A flat board, usually plumb, at the outer face of the cornice.

Flashing   Sheet metal or other material used to seal joints between masonry and wood framing, or between masonry and roofing.

Flue   The passage in a chimney through which smoke and fumes exhaust.

Footing   A masonry structure that supports a foundation wall or pier.

Foundation   The supporting structure below the first-floor construction.

Frost line   The depth of frost penetration in soil.

Furring   Wooden or metal strips applied to a wall or other surface to make a base for finish material.

Gable   The triangular wall in a house, above the eave line and within the area enclosed by the rafters.

Girder   A horizontal structural member that supports joists or a wall.

Header   A beam placed perpendicular to joists in framing for fireplace, chimney or other opening; or a wooden lintel built over openings.

Heart wood   The wood extending from the pith to the sapwood in a tree.

Hewing   To square or otherwise shape a piece of wood by chopping; as with an adze, broadaxe or other cutting tool.

Jamb   The side and overhead linings of a doorway, window or other wall opening.

Joist   A horizontal structural member that supports a floor or ceiling.

Kerf   The groove left in a piece of wood after a saw has passed through it.

Lintel   A horizontal structural member that spans any opening in a wall.

Molding   A wood strip milled for decorative trim.

Mortise   A slot cut into a log, board or timber, to receive the tenon of another member to form a joint.

Partition   A wall that divides spaces within a house.

Pier   A column of masonry used to support other structural members.

Pitch   The slope of a roof, expressed as a ratio of the total rise to the total width of a house. For example, a 10-foot rise and 30-foot width is a one-third pitch roof.

Plate   A horizontal structural member that ties together the upper ends of vertical members; as the plate across the top of wall studs. Also the top log or other member of a wall.

Plumb   Exactly vertical.

Plumb cut   A cut that runs vertical in any member that is angled; as the plumb cut on a rafter.

Plywood   A piece of wood formed of thin layers of wood glued together.

Preservative   Any substance that inhibits the growth and activity of molds, fungi, bacteria and insects in wood for a period of time.

Rafter   A structural member that supports the roof.

Rake   The trim that is applied to the edge of a roof on the gable end.

Reinforcing   Steel rods or steel mesh installed in concrete to increase strength.

Ridge piece   (also "ridge board" or "ridge pole") The structural member that ties the tops of rafters together.

Rise   The vertical height of a roof or run of stairs. The height of one step in a stair.

Riser   A vertical board closing the space between stair treads.

Roof sheathing   The plywood or other material fastened to rafters, on which the roofing is laid.

Run   The horizontal distance covered by a rafter from wall to ridge; or by a flight of stairs. The net width of a stair tread.

Sapwood   The outer layer of wood, next to the bark of a tree. In most species, it is lighter colored than heartwood.

Scribe   To cut material so that it fits an adjoining irregular surface; as in fitting wallboard or trim to logs or masonry.

Seasoning   Removing moisture from green wood to reduce its weight and improve its usefulness.

Shake   A split or sawed wood shingle.

Shingles   Roof covering of asphalt, wood, tile or other material in uniform length, width and thickness.

Shoe   The horizontal member that ties together the lower ends of studs in a wall.

Still   The horizontal base framing member of a structure. The member forming the lower side of an opening.

Slab   A foundation that incorporates a concrete floor laid on the ground.

Snow block   The material used to enclose the space between rafters, to seat against the top of the wall and the underside of roof sheathing.

Soffit   The material that encloses the underside of a cornice.

Span   The distance between structural supports.

Spline   A thin piece of material placed in grooves of two adjoining surfaces to form a joint.

Stud   A vertical framing member in walls and partitions.

Subfloor   Boards or plywood laid on joists over which finished flooring is placed.

Termite shield   A metal protection placed below wood members to prevent entry by small wood-eating insects.

Tongue-and-grooved   Material milled with a groove on one edge or side and a corresponding tongue on the other, to form an interlocking joint.

Truss   A structural member designed of several parts, to span long distances so that mainly longitudinal stresses are placed on the parts of the truss.

Vapor barrier   A material that inhibits the passage of water vapor from the inside of a house to the insulating material in walls and ceilings.

INDEX

Other SUCCESSFUL Books

SUCCESSFUL PLANTERS, Orcutt. "Definitive book on container gardening." *Philadelphia Inquirer.* Build a planter, and use it for a room divider, a living wall, a kitchen herb garden, a centerpiece, a table, an aquarium—and don't settle for anything that looks homemade! Along with construction steps, there is advice on the best types of planters for individual plants, how to locate them for best sun and shade, and how to provide the best care to keep plants healthy and beautiful, inside or outside the home. 8½"x 11"; 136 pp; over 200 photos and illustrations. Cloth $12.00. Paper $4.95.

BOOK OF SUCCESSFUL FIREPLACES, 20th ed., Lytle. The expanded, updated edition of the book that has been a standard of the trade for over 50 years—over a million copies sold! Advice is given on selecting from the many types of fireplaces available, on planning and adding fireplaces, on building fires, on constructing and using barbecues. Also includes new material on wood as a fuel, woodburning stoves, and energy savings. 8½"x 11"; 128 pp; over 250 photos and illustrations. $5.95 Paper.

SUCCESSFUL ROOFING & SIDING, Reschke. "This well-illustrated and well-organized book offers many practical ideas for improving a home's exterior." *Library Journal.* Here is full information about dealing with contractors, plus instructions specific enough for the do-it-yourselfer. All topics, from carrying out a structural checkup to supplemental exterior work like dormers, insulation, and gutters, fully covered. Materials to suit all budgets and home styles are reviewed and evaluated. 8½"x 11"; 160 pp; over 300 photos and illustrations. $5.95 Paper. (Main selection Popular Science and McGraw-Hill Book Clubs)

PRACTICAL & DECORATIVE CONCRETE, Wilde. "Spells it all out for you...is good for beginner or talented amateur..." *Detroit Sunday News.* Complete information for the layman on the use of concrete inside or outside the home. The author—Executive Director of the American Concrete Institute—gives instructions for the installation, maintenance, and repair of foundations, walkways, driveways, steps, embankments, fences, tree wells, patios, and also suggests "fun" projects. 8½"x11"; 144 pp; over 150 photos and illustrations. $12.00 Cloth. $4.95 Paper. (Featured alternate, Popular Science and McGraw-Hill Book Clubs)

SUCCESSFUL HOME ADDITIONS, Schram. For homeowners who want more room but would like to avoid the inconvenience and distress of moving, three types of home additions are discussed: garage conversion with carport added; bedroom, bathroom, sauna addition; major home renovation which includes the addition of a second-story master suite and family room. All these remodeling projects have been successfully completed and, from them, step-by-step coverage has been reported of almost all potential operations in adding on to a home. The straightforward presentation of information on materials, methods, and costs, as well as a glossary of terms, enables the homeowner to plan, arrange contracting, or take on some of the work personally in order to cut expenses. 8½"x11"; 144 pp; over 300 photos and illustrations. Cloth $12.00. Paper $5.95.

FINISHING OFF, Galvin. A book for both the new-home owner buying a "bonus space" house, and those who want to make use of previously unused areas of their homes. The author advises which jobs can be handled by the homeowner, and which should be contracted out. Projects include: putting in partitions and doors to create rooms; finishing off floors and walls and ceilings; converting attics and basements; designing kitchens and bathrooms, and installing fixtures and cabinets. Information is given for materials that best suit each job, with specifics on tools, costs, and building procedures. 8½"x11"; 144 pp; over 250 photos and illustrations. Cloth $12.00. Paper $5.95.

SUCCESSFUL FAMILY AND RECREATION ROOMS, Cornell. How to best use already finished rooms or convert spaces such as garage, basement, or attic into family/recreation rooms. Along with basics like lighting, ventilation, plumbing, and traffic patterns, the author discusses "mood setters" (color schemes, fireplaces, bars, etc.) and finishing details (flooring, wall covering, ceilings, built-ins, etc.) A special chapter gives quick ideas for problem areas. 8½"x11"; 144 pp; over 250 photos and diagrams. (Featured alternate for McGraw-Hill Book Clubs.) $12.00 Cloth. $4.95 Paper.

SUCCESSFUL HOME GREENHOUSES, Scheller. Instructions, complete with diagrams, for building all types of greenhouses. Among topics covered are: site location, climate control, drainage, ventilation, use of sun, auxiliary equipment, and maintenance. Charts provide characteristics and requirements of plants and greenhouse layouts are included in appendices. "One of the most completely detailed volumes of advice for those contemplating an investment in a greenhouse." *Publishers Weekly.* 8½"x11"; 136 pp; over 200 photos and diagrams. (Featured alternates of the Popular Science and McGraw-Hill Book Clubs). $12.00 Cloth. $4.95 Paper.

SUCCESSFUL SPACE SAVING AT HOME, Galvin. The conquest of inner space in apartments, whether tiny or ample, and homes, inside and out. Storage and built-in possibilities for all living areas, with a special section of illustrated tips from the professional space planners. 8½"x11"; 128 pp; over 150 B-W and color photographs and illustrations. $12.00 Cloth. $4.95 Paper.

SUCCESSFUL KITCHENS, 2nd ed., Galvin. Updated and revised edition of the book *Workbench* called "A thorough and thoroughly reliable guide to all phases of kitchen design and construction. Special features include how to draw up your own floor plan and cabinet arrangement, plus projects such as installing countertops, dishwashers, cabinets, flooring, lighting, and more. 8½"x11"; 144 pp; over 250 photos and illustrations, incl. color. Cloth $12.00. Paper $5.95.

SUCCESSFUL LIVING ROOMS, Hedden. A collection of projects to beautify and add enjoyment to living and dining areas. The homeowner will be able to build a bar, dramatize lighting, enhance or brighten up an old fireplace, build entertainment centers, and make structural changes. "The suggestions…are imaginative. A generous number of illustrations make the book easy to understand. Directions are concisely written…new ideas, superior presentation." *Library Journal.* 8½"x11"; 152 pp; over 200 illustrations and photos, incl. color. Cloth $12.00. Paper $5.95.

SUCCESSFUL LANDSCAPING, Felice. Tips and techniques on planning and caring for lawns, trees, shrubs, flower and vegetable gardens, and planting areas. "Profusely illustrated…this book can help those looking for advice on improving their home grounds. Thorough details." *Publishers Weekly.* "Comprehensive handbook." *American Institute of Landscape Architects.* Also covers building fences, decks, bird baths and feeders, plus climate-and-planting schedules, and a glossary of terms and chemical products. 8½"x11"; 128 pp; over 200 illustrations including color; $12.00 Cloth. $4.95 Paper.

IMPROVING THE OUTSIDE OF YOUR HOME, Schram. This complete guide to an attractive home exterior at low cost covers every element, from curb to chimney to rear fence. Emphasis is on house facade and attachments, with tips on enhancing natural settings and adding manmade features. Basic information on advantages or disadvantages of materials plus expert instructions make it easy to carry out repairs and improvements that increase the home's value and reduce its maintenance. 8½"x11"; 168 pp; over 250 illustrations including color; $12.00 Cloth. $5.95 Paper.

SUCCESSFUL LOG HOMES, Ritchie. Log homes are becoming increasingly popular—low cost, ease of construction and individuality being their main attractions. This manual tells how to work from scratch whether cutting or buying logs—or how to remodel an existing log structure—or how to build from a prepackaged kit. The author advises on best buys, site selection, evaluation of existing homes, and gives thorough instructions for building and repair. 8½"x11"; 168 pp; more than 200 illustrations including color. $12.00 Cloth. $5.95 Paper.

SUCCESSFUL SMALL FARMS—BUILDING PLANS & METHODS, Leavy. A comprehensive guide that enables the owner of a small farm to plan, construct, add to, or repair buildings at least expense and without disturbing his production. Emphasis is on projects the farmer can handle without a contractor, although advice is given on when and how to hire work out. Includes basics of farmstead layout, livestock housing, environmental controls, storage needs, fencing, building construction and preservation, and special needs. 8½"x11"; 192 pp; over 250 illustrations. $14.00 Cloth. $5.95 Paper.

SUCCESSFUL HOME REPAIR—WHEN *NOT* TO CALL THE CONTRACTOR. Anyone can cope with household repairs or emergencies using this detailed, clearly written book. The author offers tricks of the trade, recommendations on dealing with repair crises, and step-by-step repair instructions, as well as how to set up a preventive maintenance program. 8½"x11"; 144 pp; over 150 illustrations. $12.00 Cloth. $4.95 Paper.

OUTDOOR RECREATION PROJECTS, Bright. Transform you backyard into a relaxation or game area—without enormous expense—using the instructions in this book. There are small-scale projects such as putting greens, hot tubs, or children's play areas, plus more ambitious ventures including tennis courts and skating rinks. Regional differences are considered; recommendations on materials, construction methods are given as are estimated costs. "Will encourage you to build the patio you've always wanted, install a tennis court or boat dock, or construct playground equipment…Bright provides information on choosing tools, selecting lumber, and paving with concrete, brick or stone." *House Beautiful.* (Featured alternate Popular Science and McGraw-Hill Book Clubs). 8½"x11"; 160 pp; over 200 photos and illustrations including color. $12.00 Cloth. $5.95 Paper.

SUCCESSFUL WOOD BOOK—HOW TO CHOOSE, USE, AND FINISH EVERY TYPE OF WOOD, Bard. Here is the primer on wood—how to select it and use it effectively, efficiently, and safely—for all who want to panel a wall, build a house frame, make furniture, refinish a floor, or carry out any other project involving wood inside or outside the home. The author introduces the reader to wood varieties and their properties, describes major wood uses, advises on equipping a home shop, and covers techniques for working with wood including the use of paints and stains. 8½"x11"; 160 pp; over 250 illustrations including color. $12.00 Cloth. $5.95 Paper.

SUCCESSFUL PET HOMES, Mueller. "There are years worth of projects…The text is good and concise—all around, I am most impressed." *Roger Caras, Pets and Wildlife, CBS.* "A thoroughly delightful and helpful book for everyone who loves animals." *Syndicated reviewer, Lisa Oglesby.* Here is a new approach to keeping both pet owners and pets happy by choosing, buying, building functional but inexpensive houses, carriers, feeders, and play structures for dogs, cats, and birds. The concerned pet owner will find useful advice on providing for pet needs with the least wear and tear on the home. 8½"x11"; 116 pp; over 200 photos and illustrations. Cloth $12.00. $4.95 Paper.

HOW TO BUILD YOUR OWN HOME, Reschke. Construction methods and instructions for woodframe ranch, one-and-a-half story, two-story, and split level homes, with specific recommendations for materials and products. 8½"x11"; 336 pages; over 600 photographs, illustrations, and charts. (Main selection for McGraw-Hill's Engineers Book Club and Popular Science Book Club) $14.00 Cloth. $5.95 Paper.

BOOK OF SUCCESSFUL HOME PLANS. Published in cooperation with Home Planners, Inc.; designs by Richard B. Pollman. A collection of 226 outstanding home plans, plus information on standards and clearances as outlined in HUD's *Manual of Acceptable Practices*. 8½"x11";192 pp; over 500 illustrations. $12.00 Cloth. $4.95 Paper.

HOW TO CUT YOUR ENERGY BILLS, Derven and Nichols. A homeowner's guide designed not for just the fix-it person, but for everyone. Instructions on how to save money and fuel in all areas—lighting, appliances, insulation, caulking, and much more. If it's on your utility bill, you'll find it here. 8½"x11"; 136 pp; over 200 photographs and illustrations. $4.95 Paper.

WALL COVERINGS AND DECORATION, Banov. Describes and evaluates different types of papers, fabrics, foils and vinyls, and paneling. Chapters on art selection, principles of design and color. Complete installation instructions for all materials. 8½"x11"; 136 pp; over 150 B-W and color photographs and illustrations. $12.00 Cloth. $4.95 Paper.

BOOK OF SUCCESSFUL PAINTING, Banov. Everything about painting any surface, inside or outside. Includes surface preparation, paint selection and application, problems, and color in decorating. "Before dipping brush into paint, a few hours spent with this authoritative guide could head off disaster." *Publishers Weekly*. 8½"x11"; 114 pp; over 150 B-W and color photographs and illustrations. $12.00 Cloth. $4.95 Paper.

BOOK OF SUCCESSFUL BATHROOMS, Schram. Complete guide to remodeling or decorating a bathroom to suit individual needs and tastes. Materials are recommended that have more than one function, need no periodic refinishing, and fit into different budgets. Complete installation instructions. 8½"x11"; 128 pp; over 200 B-W and color photographs. (Chosen by Interior Design, Woman's How-to, and Popular Science Book Clubs) $12.00 Cloth. $4.95 Paper.

TOTAL HOME PROTECTION, Miller. How to make your home burglarproof, fireproof, accidentproof, termiteproof, windproof, and lightningproof. With specific instructions and product recommendations. 8½"x11"; 124 pp; over 150 photographs and illustrations. (Chosen by McGraw-Hill's Architects Book Club) $12.00 Cloth. $4.95 Paper.

BOOK OF SUCCESSFUL SWIMMING POOLS, Derven and Nichols. Everything the present or would-be pool owner should know, from what kind of pool he can afford and site location, to construction, energy savings, accessories and maintenance and safety. 8½"x11"; over 250 B-W and color photographs and illustrations; 128 pp. $12.00 Cloth. $4.95 Paper.

FINDING & FIXING THE OLDER HOME, Schram. Tells how to check for tell-tale signs of damage when looking for homes and how to appraise and finance them. Points out the particular problems found in older homes, with instructions on how to remedy them. 8½"x11"; 160 pp; over 200 photographs and illustrations. $4.95 Paper.

SUCCESSFUL STUDIOS AND WORK CENTERS, Davidson. How and where to set up work centers at home for the proessional or amateur—for art projects, photography, sewing, woodworking, pottery and jewelry, or home office work. The author covers equipment, floor plans, basic light/plumbing/wiring requirements, and adds interviews with artists, photographers, and other professionals telling how they handled space and work problems. 8½"x11"; 144 pp; over 200 photographs and diagrams. $12.00 Cloth. $4.95 Paper.